Acclaim for *When the Harps Went Still*

"It is a great pity that most Christians are unaware of the great musical heritage that Christianity has produced over the centuries. Church music is studied, heard, even cherished by many, but seldom is it used in its proper context. Anyone who has been to a sung Mass, with Gregorian chant and perhaps also some Renaissance polyphony, will appreciate the depth of this tragedy. With notable exceptions, the last several decades have witnessed a debasement of musical sensibilities and a squandering of musical traditions among Catholics and Protestants alike. It is not just the neglect of the great religious works of Mozart and Haydn, Bach and Beethoven, Josquin and Palestrina, or even Gregorian chant; it is their displacement by musical kitsch that often conveys questionable theology and unbridled subjectivism, if not self-praise. *When the Harps Went Still* is the latest telling of the story of 'what went wrong' with Catholic Church music. Its authors provide a panoramic view of magisterial teaching on sacred music (which, while not infallible, is informed and authoritative), seasoned with wisdom drawn from their own professional backgrounds; their method follows the principle, *Qui distinguit, bene docet* (He who makes distinctions teaches well). We are not dealing with 'mere aesthetics' here, for there is nothing 'mere' about the beautiful. If the good, the true, and the beautiful are so interwoven that to degrade one is to degrade the others, then this book is an antidote to spiritual poison."

—***Fr. Thomas Kocik,*** Member, The Society for Catholic Liturgy, Author, *The Reform of the Reform? A Liturgical Debate* and *Singing His Song: A Short Introduction to the Liturgical Movement*

I0869439

"In *When the Harps Went Still*, Maestro Aurelio Porfiri, Bishop Athanasius Schneider, and Professor Guido Milanese provide a rich synthesis of papal documents that witness to the beauty of Gregorian chant and liturgical Latin. Although Vatican II's constitution *Sacrosanctum Concilium* praised the musical tradition of the universal Church as 'a treasure of inestimable value,' the decades following the Council brought about a lamentable decline in sacred music. The authors examine the theological, liturgical, and cultural reasons for this decline, and they explain what is needed to bring about a revival of sacred music directed to the elevation of souls."

—***Robert Fastiggi,*** Ph.D., Professor of Dogmatic Theology, Sacred Heart Major Seminary, Detroit, MI

When the Harps Went Still

Aurelio Porfiri – Athanasius Schneider – Guido Milanese

WHEN THE HARPS WENT STILL

The Tragic Decline of Catholic Sacred Music

Translated by Nicholas Reitzug

SOPHIA INSTITUTE PRESS
Manchester, New Hampshire

Cover by Updatefordesign Studio
Cover image: *Ancient chapel with stained glass and altar* (FreePik, vecstock); *Grungy musical background* (Shutterstock 29164051)

Sophia Institute Press
Box 5284, Manchester, NH 03108
1-800-888-9344
www.SophiaInstitute.com

Sophia Institute Press® is a registered trademark of Sophia Institute.

paperback ISBN 978-1-64413-900-4

ebook ISBN 978-1-64413-901-1

Library of Congress Control Number: 2024946121

First printing

Contents

When the Harps Went Still

WHAT IS SACRED MUSIC?

WE LIVE IN a time of great upheavals, a time in which we have had to face a pandemic, new wars, and crippling energy crises. It seems we have never lived through such difficult times, and we try to imagine the future without giving way to desperation and systematic pessimism. Ominous predictions appear in newspaper columns, hinting at the possibility of a nuclear war that could destroy the human race. Others suggest that irreversible climate change could cause a similar mass die-off.

In a global context like our own, the question regarding the reasonableness of certain lines of reflection is not without foundation. What use is it, in a world fractured and desperate, to debate the status of art, literature, and music? And how reasonable can it be to put forth a study on Catholic sacred music, which necessarily concerns an ever-smaller minority of people, those who still attend church, and in reality a minority of this minority? Is this not an irrelevant topic, whether in the context of general culture or within the Catholic world, which seems increasingly consumed by interests of a humanitarian nature, leaving on the margins the content of revelation? And therefore necessarily marginalizing the liturgy as well, which is a direct expression of properly religious reality, and with it sacred music, which represents in turn the expression of the liturgy? It would seem, in essence, that there are more important issues with which to concern ourselves, even within the Catholic world.

In fact, the importance of sacred music, although it might not appear so at first glance, is quite considerable, and can play an almost revelatory role in the current cultural and religious situation in the formerly Catholic West. Reflection on sacred music, and on the profound crisis in which we find it, allows us to understand the reasons for the decline of the sacred in general, and the waning of religion and of those perennial religious values that have formed us. It allows us to understand why man seems plunged into a decadence that has roots firmly planted in the past. The crisis in sacred music concerns all of us as human beings: we hope that after having read this book this might be quite clear. Investigating sacred music means digging into the foundations upon which our civilization rests, looking into the depths of the decline of our Western society in the collapse of some of its load-bearing elements. The crisis of sacred music is not merely a matter of musical aesthetics, but sheds light on fundamental aspects of the current crisis of the West, in particular of the crisis of the Catholic Church.

Above all, what is sacred music? The answer to this question is both simple and complex; the very term *sacred music* presents problems, but we shall return to this in the following chapter. To give at least a provisional working definition to the object of our discussion, we might define sacred music as the music appropriate to liturgical worship, the music that forms an inseparable element of worship.[1] Sacred music is not something "other" or accessory with respect to worship but constitutes an intrinsic part of it. John of Salisbury (1120–1180), a great intellectual of medieval England, secretary of Thomas Becket, and later bishop of Chartres, offers us an interesting reason why sacred music was introduced into worship: "Therefore, the holy Fathers, when they were

1 A distinction between the broader concept of sacred music and the more specific one of liturgical music shall be offered in the following chapters.

spreading reverence in churches, reckoned not only the singing of men but also the modes of instruments to be applied in the instruction of morals and in the elevation of souls with the exultation of virtue unto the worship of the Lord." The medieval text was quoted, in 1749, by Pope Benedict XIV in his encyclical *Annus Qui Hunc*, dedicated to the upkeep of churches and to the dignity of the liturgy and sacred music.[2] John of Salisbury affirms, then, that the aim of sacred music is the "exultation of virtue" and the "elevation of souls ... unto the worship of the Lord."

This idea of "elevation of souls" offers us a very beautiful image, affirming that music has a power that surpasses that of the mere word; where the simple word is not effective, music adds a dimension that is decisive in winning souls to the Lord. This idea is frequently found throughout the history of the Magisterium, from Leo XIII to St. Pius X, to all the popes of the twentieth century, as well as in the Second Vatican Council's decree on the liturgy, *Sacrosanctum Concilium* (chapter VI). The first twentieth-century expression of this exigency is found in the *motu proprio* of St. Pius X of November 22, 1903, on sacred music, *Tra le sollecitudini*, paragraph 1, in which he defines sacred music as follows:

> Sacred music, being a complementary part of the solemn liturgy, participates in the general scope of

2 Ioannes Sarisberiensis, *Policraticus*, I 6, ed. Keats-Rohan, *CCCM* 118: *Ad mores itaque instruendos et animos exultatione virtutis traiciendos in cultum Domini non modo concentum hominum sed et instrumentorum modos censuerunt sancti patres Domino applicandos, cum templi reverentiam dilatarent.* The encyclical *Annus Qui Hunc* of Benedict XIV quotes the text of John of Salisbury in chapter 5 of the encyclical, found in Latin at https://cappellagregoriana.files.wordpress.com/2017/09/annus-qui-hunc-lt.pdf and in English at https://www.papalencyclicals.net/ben14/annus-qui-hunc.htm.

> the liturgy, which is the glory of God and the sanctification and edification of the faithful. It contributes to the decorum and the splendor of the ecclesiastical ceremonies, and since its principal office is to clothe with suitable melody the liturgical text proposed for the understanding of the faithful, its proper aim is to add greater efficacy to the text, in order that through it the faithful may be the more easily moved to devotion and better disposed for the reception of the fruits of grace belonging to the celebration of the most holy mysteries.[3]

We notice here the return of the idea of the greater power that music holds when compared to the bare text, but we also see that the liturgy must radiate with beauty and not merely be a sterile rite and purely functional. Throughout the centuries, the Church has always given the highest value to beauty in liturgical expressions because she knows that beauty constitutes the primary means for drawing people toward God.[4] Attracting the world to God, or better yet, bringing individuals to God, is the essential task that falls to the Church. Other tasks, such as the Church's social and political activities, are certainly positive and work for the good of the world, but many such activities can be carried out with equal efficacy by purely secular organizations, such as non-governmental organizations and charities, while the task the Church has received from

[3] English: https://adoremus.org/1903/11/tra-le-sollecitudini/.

[4] Besides the many interventions of the Church and the powerful reflections of Joseph Ratzinger on this point (e.g., Ratzinger's short discourse in 2006), it is appropriate to cite the refined analyses of a great contemporary philosopher, the Anglican Roger Scruton: see Scruton 2009.

her divine Founder is that of "baptizing all nations"—in other words, attracting the world to God (see Matt. 28:19).

The Church was founded by Jesus Christ to bring souls to God. The liturgy is the privileged place in which this must occur, in parallel with the transmission of doctrine. According to an ancient saying of the Church, the liturgy establishes doctrine in a certain sense: liturgical action is not indifferent to the content of the Faith, but in altering the liturgy the content of the Faith is altered in an imperceptible manner to most, though efficaciously over a long period.[5] One can deduce from this, therefore, that whatever is removed from the liturgy is removed from evangelization as well. Sacred music is internal to the liturgical action: it does not constitute a fortuitous ornament of it, but represents a full expression that arrives where the merely pronounced word cannot reach. Thus, we can derive from this that vigilance over sacred music is particularly important. Among the other instructions contained in the *motu proprio* of St. Pius X quoted above, there is the following:

> In the ordinary lessons of Liturgy, Morals, and Canon Law given to the students of theology, let care be taken to touch on those points which regard more directly the principles and laws of sacred

[5] The formula according to which liturgical practice "regulates" the content of the Faith derives from a passage of Prospero of Aquitaine, *Indiculus de Gratia Dei (Capitula Caelestini)*, 8 (PL 51, 209: a modern critical edition has yet to be made): *Ut legem credendi lex statuat supplicandi*: "Thus the law of the liturgy establishes the law of belief." This text is often translated poorly and merits proper study; see Lang 2022, p. 313 n. 18. Among previous studies, Clerck 1994 and more recently Hwang 2010, p. 82, have limited the meaning of the formula to the interpretation of a certain New Testament passage.

> music, and let an attempt be made to complete the doctrine with some particular instruction in the aesthetic side of sacred art, so that clerics may not leave the seminary ignorant of all those subjects so necessary to a full ecclesiastical education. (no. 26)

Thus, sacred music must (or ought to) be presented to seminarians in such a way that they can comprehend its importance to the liturgy: sacred music, according to the pope, should constitute a normal part of the education of the clergy, parallel to an at least elementary education in sacred art. The precise disposition of the pope should be noticed in the same document, in which he instructs "persons thoroughly competent in sacred music" to accompany, in the various dioceses, the process of improving the artistic (and thus liturgical and spiritual) level of this art (no. 24). These requests, though certainly not completely in practice even at the time of the publication of the papal document, are currently entirely forgotten. The result is that the clergy normally receive no musical education whatsoever, nor even artistic education. The result of this ignorance is that most priests who completed their studies in recent decades have no idea what sacred music might be, and are consequently not able to comprehend its meaning and function.

The random nature perceived in Catholic sacred music reminds one of Newman's observation more than a century and a half ago regarding the Anglican clergy of his time. If one speaks with one Catholic priest or another, said Newman, one is not led to notice doctrinal differences, while among Anglican clergy there reigns the most confused disparity of panoramas, which led him to ask: *Does an Anglican faith truly exist?* Newman also observed that the Anglican liturgy of his time was characterized by continuous changes, and by a chaotic doing and undoing that was the exact opposite of the stability found in Catholic liturgy and faith.

> I understand what a Catholic means by saying that he goes by the voice of the Church; it means, practically, by the voice of the first priest he meets. Every priest is the voice of the Church. This is quite intelligible. In matters of doctrine, he has faith in the word of any priest. But what, and where, is that "word" of the Church which the persons you speak of believe in? And when do they exercise their belief? Is it not true that Anglican clergymen are never in agreement among themselves on questions of faith, and what the first affirms, the second will deny? In this way, the Anglican cannot, even if he wanted to, believe in them, and must necessarily, though he would not, choose between them. How, then, has faith a place in the religion of an Anglican?[6]

From this, one can see the essential value of the education of the clergy in liturgy and sacred music: without it, the result is the present confusion, where one can never be certain upon entering a new church whether one will find a liturgy celebrated with due respect or a continuous, anxious exhibition of "liturgical creativity"—in other words, amateurish confusion. Sacred music has fallen victim to all this confusion, which is due to ignorance, on one hand, and to the loss of faith on the other that, as Joseph Ratzinger observed for decades, is both a cause and an effect of

[6] The quote is taken from Newman 2012, p. 381. On Newman and music, Milanese 2014, p. 29, offers bibliography and analysis.

the liturgical crisis. In particular, the fragmentation denounced by Newman as a characteristic of the Church of England in his time characterizes the music practice in Catholic churches today. Moreover, the choice of music employed in the liturgy often becomes an ideological weapon, chosen to represent the dominance of a faction rather than being presented as the *vox Ecclesiae* in the service of God and the conversion of the faithful.

This happens because, as in all art forms, just as music attracts us to the good, so too can it attract us to evil—if it is not truly sacred, that is. Music is never neutral, and this holds true for sacred music as well as secular music. Music has a power that can be directed toward evil as readily as toward good; this aspect must not be underestimated when considering sacred music and all the music that is used in the present age in the liturgy, however profoundly unworthy it is to be used in the liturgical action. One dedicated to sacred music knows that it must guide souls toward the good; when it does not fulfill this aim, it cannot be properly termed sacred.

In the beauty and splendor of sacred music we see the reflection of God's own beauty, that intuition of an expressive exigency that is always beyond our human capacities and that every artist perceives (whether a painter, a musical composer, a writer, a singer or one who plays an instrument), to which the text of Karol Wojtyła below testifies. We have seen how it exists *in primis* for the glory of God and secondarily for the edification of the faithful: God must be placed once more in the center, as already stated in *The Catholic Mass*. We must not dethrone God from the place that is His due. For this reason it is truly important to pay attention to the fact that God must be honored fittingly and not through second-rate creations unworthy of His glory. We recall Roger Scruton, who observed a downright expulsion of beauty from contemporary culture: the liturgy seems to be ashamed of beauty, and sacred music (which is the highest expression of the liturgy) cannot resist following its direction. The utilitarian vision that has taken hold (namely, that the liturgy is only "good" for *doing* things) has rendered impossible the true task of sacred music, which is that of opening the spirit and the mind to the fulfillment of one's full humanity.

It is often thought today that all types of music are acceptable in Catholic liturgy, on the simple condition that it utilize a biblical text, a text of a generically religious nature, or at least something vaguely spiritual. One must not forget that the texts themselves are often unworthy of entering the liturgical action due to their frequent banality and ambiguity, or to take up Ratzinger's terminology, their decidedly "horizontal" nature, which is incapable of opening us up to the transcendent.[7] Thus, music was introduced that would be more appropriate in a supermarket or an airport terminal. This was particularly evident in the "youth ministry" of the 1970s, which imposed music that was worthy, at best, of a low-quality discotheque, on the hypothesis that this adoption of worldly music would attract the wayward youth back to the Church. This did not happen , because the younger generations were abandoning the Church en masse for decades; but even more importantly, this entire project rests on a false presupposition. The question, in fact, should be: *To what are we seeking to draw the youth?* The original idea of the Liturgical Movement was to have the faithful draw close to the

7 Here too reference must be made to *Feast of Faith* as well as the lively and fascinating essay *The Spirit of the Liturgy* (Ratzinger 2001), written just a few years before Ratzinger was elevated to the papal throne. The problem of banalization also concerns the translations of the liturgy: see the classic Bianchi 2002.

wealth of the liturgy, not to lower the level of the liturgy, imagining it could be "adapted" to the mundanity of daily life, confounding this abasement with the presumed needs of the faithful. This project is very depressing, because not only does it trivialize the liturgy (which would be extremely grave *in se*), but it is grounded on a representation of the faithful as a people incapable of appreciating beauty and sacrality. In reality, today's world strongly desires to break out of the flatness of consumer society: today's man, "satiated and desperate" (using an expression from Cardinal Giacomo Biffi), perceives that hunger for what is essential and fundamental, which St. Augustine described so perfectly more than fifteen centuries ago: a hunger for fulfillment, a *cor inquietum*, which encompasses the entirety of man, always and in every age.

This profanation of the sacred has not produced any positive results: it has surrendered the liturgy and sacred music to the dullness of the quotidian, assimilating them to the bromide world and often to the negativity of violent and vulgar musical genres. Why can we not imagine that youth thirst for beauty? Have we not witnessed how youth, when things are proposed to them in an appropriate way, throw themselves into following true beauty with more enthusiasm than their elders? They themselves become witnesses to that abyss of light of which St. John Paul II spoke in his *Letter to Artists*, in which he surprised us with the following affirmations:

> Every genuine artistic intuition goes beyond what the senses perceive and, reaching beneath reality's surface, strives to interpret its hidden mystery. The intuition itself springs from the depths of the human soul, where the desire to give meaning to

> one's own life is joined by the fleeting vision of beauty and of the mysterious unity of things. All artists experience the unbridgeable gap which lies between the work of their hands, however successful it may be, and the dazzling perfection of the beauty glimpsed in the ardor of the creative moment: what they manage to express in their painting, their sculpting, their creating is no more than a glimmer of the splendor which flared for a moment before the eyes of their spirit.
>
> Believers find nothing strange in this: they know that they have had a momentary glimpse of the abyss of light which has its original wellspring in God. Is it in any way surprising that this leaves the spirit overwhelmed as it were, so that it can only stammer in reply? True artists above all are ready to acknowledge their limits and to make their own the words of the Apostle Paul, according to whom "God does not dwell in shrines made by human hands" so that "we ought not to think that the Deity is like gold or silver or stone, a representation by human art and imagination" (*Acts* 17:24, 29). If the intimate reality of things is always "beyond" the powers of human perception, how much more so is God in the depths of his unfathomable mystery![8]

For youth as for everyone, it is possible to participate in the flash of artistic creation, placing oneself in an attitude of listening to

8 Letter of John Paul II to Artists, no. 6, https://www.vatican.va/content/john-paul-ii/en/letters/1999/documents/hf_jp-ii_let_23041999_artists.html.

God, who speaks through the voice of the musician, the painter, the poet, and the philosopher. It is often said that sacred music as such should not exist, that every type of music might have *in se* the potential to be used in the liturgy. But is this true? If this were true, could we say, for example, that military music does not exist? Or could we say that pop music does not exist? Having said this, we could affirm that any type of music could become military music, on the condition that it is played during military exercises, or that Indian classical music becomes pop when it is performed in a dance club. A thorough preparation in musicology is certainly not necessary to understand that the attempt at canceling the musical tradition of the Catholic Church, probably carried out with good intentions, ended up in depriving the faithful of that nourishment that true sacred music offers by means of its beauty and the sense of adoration that fills it.

We must be careful here not to fall into a different error: that of considering sacred music to be all music that is not an immediately profane expression. Here too we must avoid falling into facile simplifications. We know well that the sacred is a broad category and that many artists are dedicated to it whose work is not strictly speaking Catholic. For Catholics, the sacred is obviously the manifestation of God, but this concept can take on many forms, more or less connected to religion. Therefore, to say that a Daoist hymn is sacred for a Catholic as well is certainly a mystifying misreading of the Catholic understanding of *sacred*. A Buddhist hymn has sacred value for those who adhere to that religious system, and it must be respected for its cultural value. But this is based on a vision of the world that is completely different from the Catholic one, and for this reason, it cannot be introduced into Catholic liturgy.

As concerns the repertoire of other Christian confessions, the issue is more complex. We cannot fail to appreciate the musical tradition of some of these communities, such as that of the Orthodox, the Anglicans, and the many contributions of Protestants. It cannot be denied that, especially concerning Anglicans and Protestants more broadly, many of their musical traditions are a direct derivation from the musical tradition of the Catholic Church. Having said this, our musical tradition offers its own specific characteristics, which must not be abandoned for the sake of entrusting the entire liturgical repertoire to the musical language of, for example, the Lutheran choral tradition. One can certainly take up what is useful and render it suitable to the Catholic liturgy, but this does not presume that the musical traditions of Lutheranism, for example, should take the place of the musical languages that the Catholic Church has developed over the course of her long history.

Defining the Object: Liturgical Music, Sacred Music, Ritual Music, Religious Music

HAVING BEGUN OUR discussion of the importance of sacred music, we must examine an important question that follows our initial observations. This concerns the name itself that we attribute to the repertoires under study. The lexical variations around this issue are vast. These repertoires have been termed in various ways: liturgical music, ritual music, Church music, religious music, sacred music, and so forth. As the Chinese philosopher Confucius wisely said, one must know how to give meanings to terms.

> Zilu asked: "If the ruler of Wei were to entrust you with the government of the country, what would be your first initiative?" The Master said: "It would certainly be to rectify the names." Zilu said: "Really? Isn't this a little farfetched? What is this rectification for?" The Master said: "How boorish can you get! Whereupon a gentleman is incompetent, thereupon he should remain silent. If the names are not correct, language is without an object. When language is without an object, no affair can be effected. When no affair can be effected, rites and music wither. When rites and music wither, punishments and penalties miss their target. When punishments and penalties miss their target, the people do not know where they stand. Therefore, whatever a gentleman conceives of, he must be able to say; and whatever he says, he must be able to do. In the matter of

> language, a gentleman leaves nothing to chance." (Confucius 2014, 13.3)

It is helpful to recall the importance of sacred music in the Old Testament. The following quote can offer us an idea of the importance that was given to the cantor of the Temple and to music in the worship of God:

> To find the first ancestor of our cantor, we can, as stated above, turn our gaze to the Jewish world. In the oldest witnesses of the Old Testament, we find important forebearers for our cantor. Consider, for example, the famous moment narrated in Exodus, in which the sea covers the Egyptian oppressors. At that moment, filled with the vision of God's power, the Israelites give vent to their joy in song. Here is the account: "Then Miriam, the prophetess, the sister of Aaron, took a timbrel in her hand; and all the women went out after her with timbrels and dancing. And Miriam sang to them: 'Sing to the Lord, for he has triumphed gloriously; the horse and his rider he has thrown into the sea!' " (Exod. 15:20–21). The prophetess Miriam thus teaches the refrain of the victory song and presents herself as song leader, as the one who leads the singing. Moses himself, the great warrior of the Hebrew people, can often be seen in this role as well. And the Lord Himself ordered him to do so: "Now, therefore, write this song, and teach it to the people of Israel; put it in their mouths, that this song may be a witness for me against the people of Israel"

(Deut. 31:19). At the Lord's order, Moses writes the hymn and teaches it to the Israelites Himself (see Deut. 31:22). And after having pronounced this solemn hymn, Deuteronomy records: "Moses came and recited all the words of this song in the hearing of the people, he and Joshua the son of Nun" (32:44). An interesting detail is pointed out in the Jerusalem Bible, namely that at this point the Septuagint inserts verse 31:22 ("Moses wrote that day this hymn and taught it to the Israelites") and in the place of *hymn*, the word *law* is substituted. It is interesting to note that the Hebrew word used in the passage in 31:22 is *shiyr*, whose meaning is "song" or "to sing." All traditions bear witness to this interpretation, from the Latin *canticum* to the Italian *canto*, to the English *song* (one must consider that this interpretation in the English tradition is present in the King James Version down to the current ones). Throughout time, we cannot fail to notice how attention given to the musical service among the Israelites was always focused and constant, and how there was great concern that the one who served as cantor was not just anyone, but had to meet strict requirements. We know that after the Ark of the Covenant was placed in the Temple, King David chose the one to whom he would entrust the musical service in the Temple (see 1 Chron. 6:16). It was said clearly that in their service, the cantor "would follow the rule established for them"; they would improvise nothing (what does this draw to mind?). All these cantors,

> often at the direct order of the king, were also called "experts in song" (see 1 Chron. 25) and were held in high esteem for the task they carried out. It is likely that, after the organization of the musical service in the temple, the role of liturgical director (I use the word that is familiar to us only to make the matter clearer) abated in favor of the "rights" of the choir and that song distinguished itself for its opulence due to the great number of its executors. I do not, however, intend to formulate any hypotheses on the music that was performed in the Temple, because even scholars of Jewish history tell us that little can be said about this subject, and that the passages found in Sacred Scripture are often interpretively opaque.[9]

It is very important to comprehend what we mean by a certain term, and above all it is important that we discover the word that is most adequate for defining an object under discussion, as it will be the reference point of our reasoning. In our case, we must say that in all the definitions that are proposed to us, there are limits and ambiguities. I believe, however, that we must choose the one that seems the most adequate, considering moreover that, since our object is ultimately supernatural, our limited earthly vocabulary will always come up short. A further linguistic aspect should also be considered: every language presents semantic areas that cannot be superimposed on the semantic areas of other languages. A lexical and semantic analysis such as the one being proposed here cannot therefore presume to resolve the

[9] Porfiri 2021.

interlinguistic problems that inevitably arise. There exist semantic areas lexicalized in ways proper to certain languages, impossible to resolve with just one translation in the passage from another language. The proposals that follow, therefore, have an indicative value, but do not presume to have universal validity.

1. Liturgical Music

One of the terms for music intended for the liturgy is, in fact, *liturgical music*. Now, this term does not seem to present any particular difficulties. St. Pius X, in his *motu proprio* on sacred music, defines the collections under study in his document with the Latin expression *musica liturgica* only on two occasions, as the title to the seventh paragraph (*De amplitudine musicae liturgicae = Range of liturgical music*) and in the following passage:

> In seminaries of clerics and in ecclesiastical institutions let the above-mentioned traditional Gregorian Chant be cultivated by all with diligence and love, according to the Tridentine prescriptions, and let the superiors be liberal of encouragement and praise toward their young subjects. In like manner let a Schola Cantorum be established, whenever possible, among the clerics for the execution of sacred polyphony and of good liturgical music (no. 25).[10]

In one case, moreover, the document speaks of *music sacra et liturgica* (no. 3). The expression *musica liturgica* is used less frequently than *musica sacra*, which seems to be the normal form used in the papal document. We also find one mention of *canto liturgico*:

[10] *Tra le sollecitudini*, https://adoremus.org/1903/11/tra-le-sollecitudini/.

> With the exception of the melodies proper to the celebrant at the altar and to the ministers, which must be always sung in Gregorian Chant, and without accompaniment of the organ, all the rest of the liturgical chant belongs to the choir of levites, and, therefore, singers in the church, even when they are laymen, are really taking the place of the ecclesiastical choir. Hence the music rendered by them must, at least for the greater part, retain the character of choral music. (no. 12)

As we see here, the document speaks of "singers in the church" (*cantores ecclesiastici*), and we shall consider this more closely below. The document evidently refers to the practice, common in that era, of entrusting solo "numbers" the parts of the text (e.g., the Gloria), assuming an operatic character that the Cecilian Movement had been keeping hostage for decades. The choir composed of laypeople was also acceptable, although, insofar as it played a ministerial role typically carried out by the clergy, it must perform music that is, "at least for the greater part" (an addition not found in the Latin), of a choral character.

Pius XI, in his *Divini Cultus Sanctitatem* (1928), speaks almost exclusively of *musica sacra*, but when referring to song calls it *canto liturgico*: for example, the pope refers to the education of the clergy in liturgical or to the formation of *scholae cantorum* and choral groups that must receive a suitable education *liturgicus cantibus* (nos. 2, 10).[11]

[11] The document is reproduced in Latin on the website of the Holy See. An English translation does not yet exist.

Therefore, we see how the epithet *liturgical*, placed next to either *musica* or *canto*, emerges from the first documents of the twentieth century that treat these questions from the authoritative point of view of the Magisterium.

2. Sacred Music

As concerns the term sacred music, *we must be clear about the use made of this term.*

In Pope Benedict XIV's 1749 encyclical *Annus Qui Hunc*, the term *sacred music* was not used; he was much more concerned with distinguishing and regulating figurative music (which the document calls "*cantus harmonicus seu musicus*," or "*canto musicale*") from Gregorian chant ("*canto ecclesiastico*"). Much of the document is dedicated (taking up with precise documentation the debate over sacred music at the time of the Council of Trent) to examining the possibility of using polyphonic music and musical instruments in the liturgy. The pope's response was to become a constant in the subsequent pronouncements of the Magisterium: what is important is that polyphonic music does not render comprehension of the text difficult (or worse, impossible). Instruments are to be used

> to strengthen in a certain manner some force of the words to the chant, that their sense be more and more instilled in the minds of the listeners, and the minds of the faithful be moved unto the contemplation of spiritual things, and be stirred towards God and the love of divine things.... But if the instruments continuously sound, and only sometimes, as nowadays is usually done, quiet down for a few moments, that they may offer a free space for the

> hearing of polyphonic modulations and pleated volleys of voices, commonly known as trills, [and if] in other respects, they overpower and overwhelm the voice of the cantors and the sound of the words, [then] the use of such instruments is in vain and useless, nay, forbidden and interdicted (no.12).[12]

At the time of Pope Lambertini, the issue of the influence of profane music on sacred music was very serious: it was the age in which the language of profane music, both theatrical and instrumental, was constantly penetrating into sacred music and even into liturgical usage. In view of the upcoming Jubilee of 1750, Pope Lambertini prepared a document addressing the bishops of the Papal States, charging them with the complete care of churches, and the correctness and nobility of worship.[13] Pope Lambertini gave particular attention and care to indicating the best types of music to be used in the churches for the Jubilee. From Benedict XIV's text, it is quite clear that his concern was not in the least limited to the singular moment, however important, of the Jubilee event: at the basis of the text is the awareness of the "exemplary" value that Rome and its liturgical and musical practices carry, and in fact must carry, with respect to the universal Church. Good liturgy and good music in Rome carry out an educational function toward the entire Church. This consideration loses none of its significance in our own age.

The temperament of the Magisterium, attentive to contamination of the sacred by the profane, in reality was always quite vigilant,

[12] An English translation is available: https://www.papalencyclicals.net/ben14/annus-qui-hunc.htm.

[13] The title of the encyclical, in fact, was *De Ecclesiarum Cultu et Nitore; De Officiorum Ecclesiasticorum et Musices Ratione, Occasione Imminentis Anni Sancti.*

even if it did not always obtain great success. This attention to keeping music sacred (in the sense that it, in some way, came from God and ought to be returned to Him) has always been a constant concern. Analysis of the historical sources, from the Middle Ages to the twentieth century, displays this permanent interest. Unfortunately, in recent decades, the distinction between sacred and profane in the music for religious rites seems to have lost nearly all its significance.

We have already cited the *motu proprio* of Pius X, which helps us to frame the context for one who must execute sacred music. In fact, St. Pius X provided criteria to assist us in identifying what can be labeled *true* sacred music. The pontiff observed that it must possess sanctity, goodness of form, and universality.[14] I believe it is important to refer to these characteristics in defining the scope of sacred music. When properly understood, this definition is still valid, and is in a certain sense more comprehensive than that of "liturgical music." In fact, where the latter properly denotes music for the liturgy, it cannot describe musical phenomena that are not intended for the rite (although they derive from it, in a certain sense). Consider the oratories, musical compositions of a broad scope in which a sacred story from Scripture or from the lives of the saints is usually told. One could never define these compositions as profane music, although neither are they religious music in the strictest sense. Furthermore, there exists a vast production of "devotional music" that is certainly not liturgical, but also not extraneous to the "sacred" dimension. Consider all the music that in the past was performed in oratories, in religious confraternities, or in processions through towns and cities:

[14] I 2: "Sacred music should consequently possess, in the highest degree, the qualities proper to the liturgy, and in particular sanctity and goodness of form, which will spontaneously produce the final quality of universality" (more compact in the Latin text: *Sanctitate, bonitate formarum quibus et universalitas oritur*).

an entire musical world that has practically disappeared today due to the widespread dissipation of religious practice. On the contrary, musical compositions that were once intended to be performed during the liturgy today are no longer considered usable for their original destination: the many Baroque Masses, for example, composed at a time in which the liturgy conceded much more space to music than can be granted today.

3. Ritual Music

Ritual music is music written with the aim of being used within a certain rite and is not independent therefrom. Like the term *liturgical music*, the notion of ritual music does not include that broader element that incorporates extra-liturgical compositions, but that cannot be placed in antithesis to the liturgy, as must be done for profane music. This is a category that must be considered in relation to religious anthropology and, to some extent, to cultural anthropology in its broadest sense. Among the currently most well-known scholars is Edward Foley, an American liturgist and musicologist and also a Capuchin friar, author of many volumes written for the broader public. Foley often refers to the concept of ritual music, for example, in his early work *Foundations of Christian Music*. To see music as part of the rite, as functional to the rite, is certainly an interpretive slant that is often correct on the substantially anthropological level, and one that can be used in the study of music in all religious cultures. Some examples can be found in Tibetan ritual musical (Crossley-Holland 1976), Daoist ritual music (Penyeh and Xinming 1992), Polynesian ritual music (Rossen 1978), or even recent archaeological discoveries regarding ancient civilizations (O'Callaghan 1983). Nevertheless, the historical development of the relationship between music and "the sacred" in the Catholic Christian world, the subject of this volume, demands a broader consideration, one that takes into account in a non-reductive manner the role of music in the life of the Church.

4. Religious Music

It is both correct and erroneous to use the term *religious music* for music destined for worship. Certainly, music for Catholic worship is music rooted in a precise religion, of which it constitutes an expressive form: there are no doubts on this point. But contrary to the terms proposed above, which might have been too restrictive, in this case we have a term that is too broad. The category of the religious can include all those musical manifestations that are *de facto* profane, but can also express some form of aspiration for the absolute, without constituting a manifestation, an expression of a vision of the Catholic world, and often not even a Christian vision.

Unfortunately, this simple analysis is completely lacking when we find, as used in some of our churches, songs that might convey aspirations to supernatural values but that are not reasonably utilizable in the context of liturgical worship nor in a devotional context. Take, for example, "Blowin' in the Wind" by Bob Dylan: this well-known composition essentially adopts the style of a secular spiritual, not without potentially spiritual overtures, maybe even remotely religious ones, but it certainly has nothing to do with Christian belief or a Catholic vision of life or liturgy. We could present many examples, taken in part from the experience of the current musical practice in churches around the world (e.g., a "sacred" use of "Blowin' in the Wind" has been documented in the Anglican world as well).[15]

[15] See the recording of the choir in St. Paul's Cathedral performing this piece: https://www.youtube.com/watch?v=pPmICAqS7IU. On the relation between Dylan's compositions and religion (or "religiosity"), see, for example, Kvaalvaag 2019.

An analogy might help: If all Italians are Europeans, not all Europeans are Italians. In the same way, all sacred music is religious music, but not all religious music is sacred music, if one adheres to the Catholic sense of sacred music. In today's culture, with its ever more markedly post-Christian character, especially in Europe, it is often suitable to speak of "spiritual music" rather than "religious music," or of music that aspires to an openness of mind and of the person toward things that lie beyond the narrow limits of consumer society, but that nevertheless are often pantheistic or universalistic. Evidently, compositions of this type, even though not rarely respectable in terms of their musical quality, have nothing to do with the needs of sacred music that we are seeking to identify in this study.

The Most Important Magisterial Documents (and a Lost One)

WE KNOW THAT as regards the liturgy, and therefore sacred music as well, the Magisterium of the Church is called to ensure that nothing unworthy is introduced into the official worship of the Church.

Sacrosanctum Concilium, the document of the Second Vatican Council that sets forth the Council's understanding of the liturgy and sacred music, established important points in this regard:

> 1. Regulation of the sacred liturgy depends solely on the authority of the Church, that is, on the Apostolic See and, as laws may determine, on the bishop.
>
> 2. In virtue of power conceded by the law, the regulation of the liturgy within certain defined limits belongs also to the various competent territorial bodies of bishops legitimately established.
>
> 3. Therefore, no other person, even a priest, may add, remove, or change anything in the liturgy on his own authority (no. 22).

Of course, this does not mean that the hierarchy can freely dispose of the liturgy, because it is bound by the Word of God and by Tradition, which is the continuation in time of the experience and wisdom of the Church. The ecclesiastical hierarchy is not, therefore, called to propose novelties continually, but rather to be custodians of the patrimony received from tradition, adding only to it incrementally, as occurs when someone who has been entrusted with money makes it yield a return on investment. Let us not forget that the meaning of *episkopos* is "inspector," someone who is vigilant and oversees—certainly not one who is called to be an inventor of ever new proposals unrelated to the experience of the past. As Beyer has observed in his studies of the history of the word *episkopos* in biblical language, the basic meaning of the word is "supervisor or custodian" (Beyer 1967, p. 756). Not that creativity is something to be despised—rather it is to be encouraged and sustained, but it must not be used in a self-referential manner, that is, as if every generation in the life of the Church would need to start all over ignoring "those who have preceded us in the sign of the faith," as the Roman Canon of the Mass says (*qui nos praecesserunt cum signo fidei*).

In our age, a nearly demiurgic conception of creativity has spread, according to which a creator is one who creates *ex nihilo*, without regard for what preceded him, and even at times against it. Creation from nothing is certainly to be attributed to God, Lord and Creator, but obviously it cannot be referred to human beings who create in a tradition, with a tradition, and for a tradition. The principle expressed by Benedict XV in 1914 in his encyclical *Ad Beatissimi Apostolorum* still merits our attentive reflection:

> Besides, the Church demands from those who have devoted themselves to furthering her interests, something very different from dwelling upon profitless questions; she demands that they should

devote the whole of their energy to preserving the faith intact and unsullied by any breath of error, and follow most closely him whom Christ has appointed to be the guardian and interpreter of the truth. There are to be found today, and in no small numbers, men, of whom the Apostle says that: "having itching ears, they will not endure sound doctrine: but according to their own desires they will heap up to themselves teachers, and will indeed turn away their hearing from the truth, but will be turned unto fables" (II *Tim.* iv. 34). Infatuated and carried away by a lofty idea of the human intellect, by which God's good gift has certainly made incredible progress in the study of nature, confident in their own judgment, and contemptuous of the authority of the Church, they have reached such a degree of rashness as not to hesitate to measure by the standard of their own mind even the hidden things of God and all that God has revealed to men. Hence arose the monstrous errors of "Modernism," which Our Predecessor rightly declared to be "the synthesis of all heresies," (*omnium haereseon collectum*), and solemnly condemned. We hereby renew that condemnation in all its fulness, Venerable Brethren, and as the plague is not yet entirely stamped out, but lurks here and there in hidden places, We exhort all to be carefully here and there in hidden places, We exhort all to be carefully on their guard against any contagion of the evil, to which we may apply the words Job used in other circumstances: "It is a fire

> that devoureth even to destruction, and rooteth up all things that spring" (Job 31:12). Nor do We merely desire that Catholics should shrink from the errors of Modernism, but also from the tendencies or what is called the spirit of Modernism. Those who are infected by that spirit develop a keen dislike for all that savors of antiquity and become eager searchers after novelties in everything: in the way in which they carry out religious functions, in the ruling of Catholic institutions, and even in private exercises of piety. Therefore it is Our will that the law of our forefathers should still be held sacred: "Let there be no innovation; keep to what has been handed down" (*Nihil innovetur, nisi quod traditum est*). In matters of faith that must be inviolably adhered to as the law; it may however also serve as a guide even in matters subject to change, but even in such cases the rule would hold: "Old things, but in a new way."[16]

Thus, *non nova sed noviter*, said Benedict XV, recalling the celebrated adage *nihil innovetur, nisi quod traditum est.* As Joseph Ratzinger observed beginning in the 1980s, the conviction became widespread that it is necessary "always to invent something," that there must always be some "creative formula, however banal it might be" (Ratzinger 1985 [47–48; 50]). A fine text by the great theologian Brunero Gherardini examines this more deeply:

[16] The text can be found at https://www.vatican.va/content/benedict-xv/en/encyclicals/documents/hf_ben-xv_enc_01111914_ad-beatissimi-apostolorum.html.

> Discernment and the guarantee of the Church as subject are the work of her Magisterium, which on one hand depends on its object, and is at its service, capable of teaching only what was revealed and as such handed down; on the other hand, it is her own magisterial activity, as well as its content, the complex of truths magisterially taught: quite rightly does one say of a certain doctrine: "this is Magisterium." In the former case, the word "Magisterium" is understood in an *active sense* of Authority that teaches within well-defined limits, beyond or against which such Authority loses vigor and significance. In the latter case, "Magisterium" has a *passive sense*, that of the truths taught, or an *instrumental sense* of the power used by the Church to perform its mandate of "mother and teacher."

The Dogmatic Constitution on divine revelation *Dei Verbum* explains in chapter 10 that the Magisterium is at the service of the Word of God and therefore declares that it is not superior to it, with respect to the primacy of revelation *in se* and as it is transmitted. The Magisterium can in fact only retransmit as definitive or "tending to be definitive" that and only that which it has first received: "*Quæcumque dixero vobis*" (John 14:26). This is the source of the ancient saying "*Nihil innovetur, nisi quod traditum est*," in which "*nisi*" does not impede the renewal, but presupposes it and seeks it homogenously with the revealed and transmitted truth. These observations help us to understand and situate the problem of the Magisterium's role and its documents in the field we are examining, and as a consequence, also the limits within which this magisterium must operate. It cannot and must not teach anything that is contrary to the constant teaching of the Church; otherwise it would cease to perform the function entrusted to it.

It is in this sense that the documents concerning liturgy and sacred music must be considered: we find in them the voice of the constant Magisterium of the Church, not tendencies imposed by fleeting trends of the world. It must be said that not all documents have the same importance, and distinctions must be made among the various teachings. For example, the documents that derive from the work of commissions of experts, though they have the pontifical guarantee, do not carry the same weight as official magisterial documents.

We do not wish to list the most important magisterial documentation regarding sacred music, for it would be inevitably incomplete. It will be helpful to offer a panorama that can indicate the important coordinates of the Catholic Church's reflection on this important aspect of her life, an aspect that, as we have said, is intimately bound to the liturgy and cannot be understood independently of it. In fact, the crisis of the liturgy clarifies the crisis of sacred music, and vice versa.

1. John XXII

First, it is helpful to mention the constitution *Docta Sanctorum Patrum* of John XXII, published in 1324. It was the age of the Avignon papacy: John XXII, like his predecessor Clement V, was French (Jacques-Arnaud Duèze), and his positions on sacred music can be understood in light of French music in that period.[17] The pope observed:

[17] On John XXII and music, see the synthesis in Berry 2001, with the previous bibliography.

> Some disciples of a new school, while they worried about the measuring of time, applied themselves to creating with new notes, melodies of their own invention rather than singing old ones. They perform ecclesiastical songs with whole notes and half notes and echo the notes: in fact, they break the melodies with hiccups (*hoquetis*), they soil them with descants, they even stuff them with triplets and motets in the vulgate to the point of despising the fundamentals of the antiphonal and the gradual and no longer knowing what to build upon; they ignore the tones and cannot distinguish them, and in fact confound them due to the great number of those notes and the modest jumps and the controlled descents of the fixed melody (*cantus firmus*) remain reciprocally obscured, but only these enable one to distinguish the tones themselves. Thus, they race ahead without stopping; they inebriate the ears and bring no catharsis; they simulate what they pronounce through external gestures; thus, they omit that devotion that should be sought and propagate the lasciviousness which, instead, should be avoided. For good reason did Boethius say, "The licentious soul either delights in licentious ways or heeding them frequently is softened and enervated."[18]

The references are clearly to the *ars nova* of that age (*nonnulli novellae scholae discipuli*), and the concern of the eighty-year-old

[18] *De Institutione Musica* I 1, p. 180 Friedlein.

pontiff was to avoid allowing the "new music," which was based on a measured rhythm (*temporibus misurandis*) and not on the verbal rhythm of the Gregorian repertoire, with voices and even a French text, as was the common practice, and with the so-called *hoquetus*.[19] The pope harkened unto the tradition of the amplification of plainsong, which did not obfuscate the original melody and allowed it to be fully perceived; he did not intend to reject the new language, but to avoid allowing music to shirk its main liturgical function. The problem seemed to lie in the perception of the text.

2. The Council of Trent

Before the Council of Trent (1545–1563), some currents of Protestantism, such as Calvinism, had almost entirely expelled music from the liturgy. In the Catholic world as well, analogous to what had happened in the Calvinist realms, there existed radical currents against polyphonic music in church. The essential points were two: 1) to differentiate the music in use in the liturgy from the language of profane music; 2) to assure that the words of the text used were not obfuscated by the music but remained perceptible. The increasingly complex writing of polyphonic music, in fact, had often rendered the words little comprehensible or entirely unintelligible. This gave rise to a legend that saw in Palestrina the savior of sacred music, because he supposedly convinced the pope at the time, Marcellus II (who was pope for only twenty-two days in 1555), to accept polyphonic music within the liturgy. The pope

[19] As concerns these characteristics, we refer the reader to any good manual on the history of late medieval music, such as Gallo 1991. Concerning the technique of the *hoquetus*, practiced at the time of Perotino and, for example, Machaut, see Sander 2001. An attentive analysis of this text is offered in Lang 2022, pp. 336–337.

was supposedly impressed by the mass that Palestrina titled *Messa per il Papa Marcello* (Mass for Pope Marcellus), characterized by a highly noble writing and the absolute comprehensibility of the text performed. This is a legend, but nevertheless it shows how controversies over sacred music reached the point, even in Catholic settings, of risking disastrous results for the fate of musical compositions (see Lang 2022, pp. 363–364, and the classics K. Fellerer and Hadas 1953 and K. G. Fellerer 1967).

Finding a balanced position was very difficult: profane music, formerly completely subjugated to sacred music, was now demanding more and more its own rights, and at a certain point its practice would prevail over sacred music, such that, if formerly profane music had been derived from sacred music, now this relationship was inverted. It was a case of not excluding music from the rite, on one hand, and on the other not allowing the profane language to suffocate the text, which, as "text," risked becoming a pretext for musical composition.

3. Benedict XIV

The assimilation of sacred music to profane language remained a problem in the following centuries as well. Where great masters like Palestrina and De Victoria composed sacred music in which the relationship between the text and the music not only is correct but is even the driving force behind their masterpieces, other musicians pushed once more toward the language of profane music, and in particular of musical theater of the period. Among the documents that attest to the difficulty of this situation, we recall the previously cited 1749 encyclical *Annus Qui Hunc* of Benedict XIV, written in view of the Jubilee year of 1750, in which Pope Lambertini was concerned to receive the pilgrims in clean, well-maintained churches, with a worthy liturgy and in particular with sacred music that would not scandalize the visitors flocking to Rome. Citing the Council of Trent as well as the *Docta Sanctorum* of John XXII, Lambertini offered an implicit lesson on the Catholic Magisterium, which situates itself, as he observed at the beginning of this chapter, within the living river of magisterial tradition, and does not consist in a self-referential exercise of power. The pope then observes:

> And finally, that we may end Our discourse concerning this matter, that is, concerning the abuse of theatrical singing in churches, which by itself has been for a long time manifest that there is no more need for words or proofs; it will suffice to indicate that all of them who were cited by Us above, as authors who favored the use of figured chant or polyphonic music and musical instruments in churches, undisguisedly acknowledge and demonstrate themselves to have made with the same mind and counsel whatsoever they have written, that by no means these may be understood to be about the singing and sound proper to stage and theater, which these and others in like manner condemn and abhor; but about the singing and sound which is becoming of churches, and which excites people unto devotion. Their intention can be known by anyone through reading their writings.[20]

Despite the words of the pope, theatrical song not only was not to be eliminated from churches [CMS 6.46], but would become

[20] *Annus Qui Hunc*, https://www.papalencyclicals.net/ben14/annus-qui-hunc.htm.

increasingly invasive, especially in the nineteenth century, a century in which opera became so popular as to constitute a sort of pan-European parlance. A reform was attempted, such as that of the celebrated musician Gaspare Spuntini, who, under the impulse of Pope Gregory XVI, wrote a *Report on the Reform of Sacred Music* (see Bassi 1994).

4. The Nineteenth Century

The most important reform impulse, however, would come from the Benedictines and in a special way from Dom Prosper Guéranger (1805–1875) and from the refoundation of the monastery of Solesmes and the Benedictine Order in France (1833), a push that would give life to what would later be called the Liturgical Movement. From the liturgical point of view, the line of Dom Guéranger was to reintroduce in France the Roman usage, abolishing the local "neo-Gallican" liturgical usages. For example, the young monk used the Roman Missal while the local clergy for the most part used the Parisian Missal. Naturally, song had an essential role in this project, due to the inseparable bond between liturgy and song. Despite numerous hurdles, Dom Guéranger's project met with success, in large part thanks to the serious, scholarly imprint he gave to his work through the recovery of the oldest manuscripts, which at first were copied by hand and later, after the advent of photography, were photocopied and archived in the Solesmes Abbey. At the center of these efforts was the restoration of Gregorian chant, which he sought to return to its ancient form.[21] This

[21] The bibliography on Guéranger and Solesmes is copious: we refer to just two quite diverse titles, one from within Solesmes and rather hagiographical (Combe 2003), the other more recent, which places the activity of Solesmes in relation to the cultural situation of the time (Bergeron 1998).

important project encountered strong hostility, but slowly obtained the approval of the Vatican. The first document that shows the interest of the Holy See in a new approach to sacred music was the work of Leo XIII. In his *Normae pro Musica Sacra* (1894), Leo XIII concluded the process of nineteenth-century unification of sacred music. The text includes all the basic concepts that would inform the official position of the Church from Pius X until Vatican II and beyond. We can summarize its content thus:

1. Recognition of Gregorian chant as belonging to the Church
2. The role of polyphony and, in a particular way, of the compositions of Palestrina
3. Preference for organ compositions of the Roman School, therefore those of Frescobaldi and other masters of his time
4. Although liturgical songs must be in Latin, in functions of a devotional nature the local language can be used
5. Rejection of theatrical music
6. The necessity of carrying out the liturgical text in a complete manner, without interrupting it or omitting sections
7. Prohibition of improvising on the organ without the necessary expertise

At the time, the controversy was quite lively, and the authoritative tone of the document shows that the pope had taken the question very seriously: all the essential concepts that would be taken up and expanded by Pius X and successive popes are found in this document.

5. St. Pius X and Pius XI

The *motu proprio, Tra le sollecitudini* of Pius X, promulgated on November 22, 1903, opened the new century. It was so important that St. Pius X spoke of it as a sort of juridical code for sacred music, and in it we find some of the principles that would become bulwarks of the liturgical movement, such as:

> That our most lively desire, in fact, that the true Christian spirit might blossom once more in every way and be maintained in all the faithful, it is necessary to supply first every other thing to sanctity and dignity of the church, where in fact the faithful gather to draw that spirit from its primary and indispensable source which is the active participation in the sacrosanct mysteries and in the public and solemn prayers of the Church. And it is vain to hope that to this end the blessing of heaven might descend upon us, when our obedience to the Most High, rather than as a tenderly rising perfume, places once more in the hand of the Lord the scourges which the Divine Redeemer used to chase the unworthy profaners from the temple. For this reason, so that no one might from now on present excuses for not knowing clearly their duty and in order to remove any uncertainty in the interpretation of some matters already commanded, we have deemed expedient to declare with brevity those

> principles that regulate sacred music in worship functions and draw together in a general framework the main prescriptions of the Church against the most common abuses in these matters.[22]

This document was to mark an entire age and would give impulse to a movement of renewal that was to see among its protagonists the Association of Santa Cecilia, founded in Germany in the mid-nineteenth century, and which later spread into many other countries.[23] The *motu proprio* would remain a reference point for successive popes, such as Pius XI, who would celebrate the twenty-fifth anniversary of its promulgation with a papal bull (*Divini Cultus*). In this, he repeated the importance of the Magisterium's vigilance in sacred matters and deplored the abuses still at large:

> It is of the utmost importance, therefore, that anything that is used to adorn the Liturgy should be controlled by the Church, so that the arts may take their proper place as most noble ministers in sacred worship. Far from resulting in a loss to art, such an arrangement will certainly make for the greater splendor and dignity of the arts that are used in the

[22] To this effect, we must observe that the *motu proprio* of St. Pius X has been used both by those who sought a restoration of sacred music and also by those who, on the other hand, within the same Liturgical Movement, have sought to force sacred music and the liturgy in a more innovative direction.

[23] Many important studies of the Association of Santa Cecilia have been recently published as well. See the well-documented works of Casadei Turroni Monti and Ruini 2004, Casadei Turroni Monti 2011, and at the convention on Giovanni Tebaldini in 2016 (Dessì and Lovato 2017).

Church. This has been especially true of sacred music. Wherever the regulations on this subject have been carefully observed, a new life has been given to this delightful art, and the spirit of religion has prospered; the faithful have gained a deeper understanding of the sacred Liturgy, and have taken part with greater zest in the ceremonies of the Mass, in the singing of the psalms and the public prayers. Of this We Ourselves had happy experience when, in the first year of Our Pontificate, We celebrated solemn High Mass in the Vatican Basilica to the noble accompaniment of a choir of clerics of all nationalities, singing in Gregorian Chant. It is, however, to be deplored that these most wise laws in some places have not been fully observed, and therefore their intended results not obtained. We know that some have declared these laws, though so solemnly promulgated, were not binding upon their obedience. Others obeyed them at first, but have since come gradually to give countenance to a type of music which should be altogether banned from our churches. In some cases, especially when the memory of some famous musician was being celebrated, the opportunity has been taken of performing in church certain works which, however excellent, should never have been performed there, since they were entirely out of keeping with the sacredness of the place and of the Liturgy.[24]

[24] An English translation is available in full: https://adoremus.org/1928/12/on-divine-worship/.

6. Pius XII

Pius XI's successor, Eugenio Pacelli, who took the name Pius XII, gave particular attention to sacred music. This attention was not out of the ordinary, given that this pope was himself a dedicated violinist. The twenty years of his pontificate were notable for the volume of teachings given to the Church in those years; those efforts, which had been initiated by St. Pius X during the anti-Modernist campaign, succeeded in making heard the voices that clamored for radical reforms in the Church, beginning with the liturgy. From this pontificate, it is important to cite the encyclical *Musicae Sacrae* of 1955. This document is completely dedicated to music in the liturgy. The pope also faces the important topic of the free inspiration of the artist and the proper deference to norms that regulate sacred art and music for liturgical worship. Pacelli observes:

> Sacred music obeys laws and rules which are no different from those prescribed for all religious art and, indeed, for art in general. Now we are aware of the fact that during recent years some artists, gravely offending against Christian piety, have dared to bring into churches works devoid of any religious inspiration and completely at variance with the right rules of art. They try to justify this deplorable conduct by plausible-looking arguments which they claim are based on the nature and character of art itself. They go on to say that artistic inspiration is free and that it is wrong to impose upon it laws and standards extraneous to art, whether they are religious or moral, since such rules seriously hurt the

dignity of art and place bonds and shackles on the activity of an inspired artist.

Arguments of this kind raise a question which is certainly difficult and serious, and which affects all art and every artist. It is a question which is not to be answered by an appeal to the principles of art or of aesthetics, but which must be decided in terms of the supreme principle of the final end, which is the inviolate and sacred rule for every man and every human act.

The ordination and direction of man to his ultimate end—which is God—by absolute and necessary law based on the nature and the infinite perfection of God Himself is so solid that not even God could exempt anyone from it. This eternal and unchangeable law commands that man himself and all his actions should manifest and imitate, so far as possible, God's infinite perfection for the praise and glory of the Creator. Since man is born to attain this supreme end, he ought to conform himself and through his actions direct all powers of his body and his soul, rightly ordered among themselves and duly subjected to the end they are meant to attain, to the divine Model. Therefore even art and works of art must be judged in the light of their conformity and concord with man's final end.

Art certainly must be listed among the noblest manifestations of human genius. Its purpose is to express in human works the infinite divine beauty of which it is, as it were, the reflection. Hence that outworn dictum "art for art's sake" entirely neglects

> the end for which every creature is made. Some people wrongly assert that art should be exempted entirely from every rule which does not spring from art itself. Thus this dictum either has no worth at all or is gravely offensive to God Himself, the Creator and Ultimate End.
>
> Since the freedom of the artist is not a blind instinct to act in accordance with his own whim or some desire for novelty, it is in no way restricted or destroyed, but actually ennobled and perfected, when it is made subject to the divine law. (nos. 22–26)

Unfortunately, the admirable exposition by this pontiff would be practically ignored in the decades to come, and the liturgy would succumb to new cultural fashions that preserve nothing of the dignity of worship that is God's due.

We must not forget that the forces that desired radical reform in the liturgy knew how to move behind the back of this pontiff with great ability. In fact, he gave room to several liturgical reforms such as that concerning Holy Week, which represented a "dress rehearsal" of the comprehensive liturgical reform that Msgr. Annibale Bugnini had planned already in 1949.[25] It is worth noting as well that the reformers knew how to use to their advantage a phrase of Pius XII pronounced in a discourse in 1956 for the Convention for Pastoral Liturgy in Assisi:

> The liturgical movement appeared as a sign of the providential dispositions of God for the present time, as the passage of the Holy Spirit in his

[25] See Bugnini 1949. Historical documentation in Milanese 2005.

> Church, to draw men closer to the mysteries of the faith and the wealth of graces unleashed by the active participation of the faithful in the liturgical life.[26]

Neither can we omit citing the Instruction of the Sacred Congregation of Rites in 1958, a month before the death of Pacelli (*Instructio de Musica Sacra et Sacra Liturgia*), in which the teaching of Pius XII on the liturgy and sacred music is condensed but which also advances some of the practical rules on the use of song in the vernacular for non-liturgical situations, but with the absolute obligation of Latin as the sole liturgical language.[27]

7. The Age of the Second Vatican Council

Pius XII was succeeded by John XXIII, a pope who certainly did not appear to be an unscrupulous innovator. Among his writings, we recall *Veterum Sapientia* of 1962, in which he reiterated the importance of Latin in the life of the Church and imposed its use in teaching at pontifical universities, observing that the use of Latin rendered all students equal regardless of their nation of origin or native language.[28] But was 1962 not the same year in which the Second Vatican Council began? Only eight months passed from the promulgation of *Veterum Sapientia* to the opening of Vatican

[26] "Le mouvement liturgique est apparu ainsi comme un signe des dispositions providentielles de Dieu sur le temps présent, comme un passage du Saint-Esprit dans son Église, pour rapprocher davantage les hommes des mystères de la foi et des richesses de la grâce, qui découlent de la participation active des fidèles à la vie liturgique."

[27] The English text can be found at https://adoremus.org/1958/09/instruction-on-sacred-music/.

[28] One can read an English translation at https://www.papalencyclicals.net/john23/j23veterum.htm.

II, but the distance between the two seems more like centuries. In fact, in 1959, John XXIII had decided to convoke an Ecumenical Council, and one of the topics to be discussed there would certainly be the liturgy and sacred music. The document that would contain the Council's dispositions on the matter of liturgy and sacred music is *Sacrosanctum Concilium*, approved on December 4, 1963. Chapter 6 of this document is entirely dedicated to sacred music and opens with these words:

> The musical tradition of the universal Church is a treasure of inestimable value, greater even than that of any other art. The main reason for this pre-eminence is that, as sacred song united to the words, it forms a necessary or integral part of the solemn liturgy.
>
> Holy Scripture, indeed, has bestowed praise upon sacred song, and the same may be said of the fathers of the Church and of the Roman pontiffs who in recent times, led by St. Pius X, have explained more precisely the ministerial function supplied by sacred music in the service of the Lord.
>
> Therefore, sacred music is to be considered the more holy in proportion as it is more closely connected with the liturgical action, whether it adds delight to prayer, fosters unity of minds, or confers greater solemnity upon the sacred rites. But the Church approves of all forms of true art having the needed qualities and admits them into divine worship.

These important words led some to hope for renewed attention to sacred music. In reality, a destructive fury would soon be unleashed, casting aside the patrimony that had just been so exalted in words.

The various Instructions that followed indicating the application of *Sacrosanctum Concilium* and in light of the new missal, promulgated in 1969, did not always bring clarity, and certainly were not able to restrain the savagery that would lead to the destruction of centuries of liturgical and musical tradition. One of these Instructions, *Musicam Sacram* of 1967, affirmed some of the notions found in the document of 1963 cited above, although in other points it could not avoid creating even greater confusion.[29]

8. After Vatican II

The pontificates following the Second Vatican Council would all be oriented toward the Council's application, and sacred music would not be the subject of any particularly important documents, although the topic emerged in the speeches of several popes particularly fond of music, such as John Paul II and Benedict XVI. This would not prevent the continual degradation of music, and today one wonders if such a document of the solemn Magisterium could even hope to change the sorry state of sacred music. Joseph Ratzinger intervened with scholarly studies as well as in official documents after his election to the papacy, and also through his liturgical example: Benedict XVI always sang correctly the parts of the Mass that called for it, despite the limits of his voice as an old man. It suffices to consider *Feast of the Faith* (Ratzinger 1986), as well as the role that music played in Ratzinger's texts, which was never marginal.

[29] See the recent Porfiri 2017 on *Musicam Sacram* and Porfiri 2021 on *Sacrosanctum Concilium*. This is not the place for a complete bibliography on the matter from the historical point of view. The reconstruction offered by Bugnini in that period is naturally based on a defense of his own handling of the situation (Bugnini 1983). Reference points in Milanese 2005.

Mention must be given to a document that never appeared concerning sacred music.[30] It was the year 1984, and John Paul II was pope. The vice president of the Pontifical Institute of Sacred Music was Dom Bonifacio Baroffio. Dom Baroffio was known as one of the greatest experts on Gregorian chant, to which he had dedicated numerous publications. One morning in the monastery of San Girolamo, where the Pontifical Institute of Sacred Music was headquartered, he was approached by a confrere who was working at the Congregation for Divine Worship, Fr. Antoine Dumas. He asked Fr. Baroffio to participate in the drafting of a document on sacred music. This was a period of assessment of the liturgical reform. This is probably what the Vatican desired, and we find it echoed in a discourse given by John Paul II on October 27 of that year to commemorate the twentieth anniversary of *Sacrosanctum Concilium*, in which he said to the participants: "Twenty years is a sufficient period of time for us to calmly reflect on the restructuring of the liturgy, as the Council understood and desired it; on its current implementation and pastoral effect; on the prospects of its full appreciation as the 'apex' of the life and action of the Church." In these analyses, the role that sacred music played in the liturgical reform was probably considered. The vice president of the Pontifical Institute of Sacred Music accepted the task, hoping it would not cost him too much time, given his already heavy workload for the institute. He was surprised when he received the letter of nomination as director of a working group that included several international experts. He then went to the Congregation on Divine Worship and spoke with the prefect, Cardinal Giuseppe Casoria, to tell him he would rather not be the

30 I thank Professor Giacomo Baroffio (who in the meantime has left the Benedictine Order) for the information he supplied me for this section concerning the document never promulgated.

director of the group, but that if he had to carry out this task he wanted the document to present a positive vision of sacred music, not a battle against this or that. The cardinal seemed to agree with the Benedictine monk. Matters did not go smoothly during the meetings, yet Dom Baroffio assigned each member of the commission the theme of a chapter; then at the end everything was examined and the supervisor made a final draft, fine-tuning everything to render it coherent. He then submitted the finished text to Fr. Diego Coletti, who lived in the monastery of San Gerolamo, to take it to the Congregation.

A month later, Dom Baroffio received a telephone call from the Congregation to inform him that they were alarmed because they had not heard from him. Thus, they had been forced to name a vice supervisor to write another text, quite different from the one that had come out of the first commission. Dom Baroffio was left quite vexed by all this. What had come of his text? He later found out that indeed, his text had been received, but it had ended up under a pile of other documents and was lost. He was asked to remain as director, and he made a series of observations on the new text (in fact, only on the first page), which he deemed inadequate. In the summer of that year, while participating in the Liturgical Week in Reggio Calabria organized by the Roman Center of Liturgical Action, he discovered that the text was about to be released. He was deeply annoyed by this news and hastily returned to Rome to consult with the prefect of the Holy Office, then Cardinal Joseph Ratzinger. He showed him the work that had been done and asked him to intervene in this regrettable situation. In the end, the document never came to light.

As stated, magisterial documents obviously count insofar as they lay down regulations for the liturgy and sacred music. A distinction must be made between documents with a greater juridical weight and other occasional pronouncements, which certainly bear importance but lack the force of official statements. Furthermore, a magisterial document interprets the Tradition of the Church for the time in which it is promulgated, thus allowing the faithful to read the signs of the times in light of the perennial Magisterium of the Church. If, in these documents, one finds something that is conspicuously opposed to the Tradition (hypothetically speaking), it would then be licit not only to doubt it but to oppose it.

The Reasons for the Crisis

IN THE PRECEDING paragraphs we were able to appreciate how sacred music has always enjoyed the solicitude of the Magisterium due to its intimate union with the liturgy; indeed, as we saw, the liturgy is inseparable from sacred music. There cannot be good liturgy with bad sacred music (or vice versa) without throwing off the entire celebration. The aim of sacred music is undoubtedly the liturgy, but it is also true that the liturgy is cloaked in beauty thanks to the contribution of song and of music in general (this refers not only to the singing of the choir but also to that of the priest and the faithful). The sung Mass—namely, the Mass in which the entire liturgy is carried out in musical form, from the simple recitative (cantillation) to the most elaborate songs—does not consist in an exhibition of this or that element of the celebration, but in the harmonization of song of the Body of Christ reunited to give glory to God, the members with its Head, who desired that "the priestly life begun with the supplication and sacrifice of His mortal body should continue without intermission down the ages in His Mystical Body which is the Church. That is why He established a visible priesthood to offer everywhere the clean oblation (Mal 1:11) which would enable men from East to West, freed from the shackles of sin, to offer God that unconstrained and voluntary homage which their conscience dictates."[31]

[31] Pius XII, *Mediator Dei*, 1947, https://www.vatican.va/content/pius-xii/en/encyclicals/documents/hf_p-xii_enc_20111947_mediator-dei.html.

Now, we must ask ourselves why there is this present crisis in sacred music. First of all, does this crisis exist? We believe it is important to support our statements with a sufficiently exhaustive explanation of the reasons why we are convinced that sacred music finds itself in a situation of grave crisis.

The Second Vatican Council, in *Sacrosanctum Concilium*, solemnly stated:

> The musical tradition of the universal Church is a treasure of inestimable value, greater even than that of any other art. The main reason for this pre-eminence is that, as sacred song united to the words, it forms a necessary or integral part of the solemn liturgy.
>
> Holy Scripture, indeed, has bestowed praise upon sacred song, and the same may be said of the fathers of the Church and of the Roman pontiffs who in recent times, led by St. Pius X, have explained more precisely the ministerial function supplied by sacred music in the service of the Lord (no. 112).

These are words of highest praise for the musical tradition of the Catholic Church; further on in the document, one reads that Gregorian chant is the type of song proper to the Roman liturgy (no. 116), that the organ "is to be held in high esteem" (no. 120), that the *scholae cantorum* should be fostered (no. 114), and so forth. But what really happened after Vatican II approved such a promising document? Things went in the opposite direction from what the Council envisioned, and a frightening crisis emerged from this: Gregorian chant, the organ, the *scholae cantorum*, the traditional music of the Catholic Church, all were opposed in a ferocious and merciless manner. And this battle has not stopped but continues even today: the devastating crisis of sacred music has certainly not come to an end. The sixty years since *Sacrosanctum Concilium*'s promulgation have witnessed a paradoxical phenomenon: hostility toward all the musical characteristics approved by the Second Vatican Council has taken root in widespread practice, such that those who defend sacred music as described by Vatican II are accused of being "anti-conciliar"—a generic accusation and obviously completely lacking in proof of any type, since it is quite simple to show that in reality the "anti-conciliar" ones are those who maintain positions in contrast with the texts of Vatican II.

We believe a sort of phenomenology of reasons is possible, which we can use to comprehend the meaning of this upheaval that struck the Church in an evident way in recent decades but that has its roots in periods long antecedent to it. There can be other reasons beyond those that we shall cite here below, but these seem to be the most representative.

1. The Theological Reason

One of the most important reasons to be considered when reflecting on the crisis of sacred music concerns theology. Oddly, we find ourselves to some degree in agreement with the current prefect of the Congregation for Divine Worship, Cardinal Arthur Roche, who suggests that the ancient Mass must be seriously restricted because today's theology has changed. Roche's observations are obviously erroneous at least from the historical point of view: the prefect maintains that in the "classical" Mass, the priest celebrant represents the entire people, whereas in the current liturgy it is not only the priest celebrant but all the baptized together with him. In reality, in *Mediator Dei*, Pius XII highlighted the fact that it was traditional doctrine (the pope cites Innocent III and Robert

Bellarmine) affirming that "what is carried out in particular through the ministry of the priests, is carried out universally by the offering of the faithful."[32] In fact, the change is of a different nature: that of putting man in God's place. If the liturgy is no longer directed to God, but is centered on man, on his desires and his aspirations, then it is no longer necessary for music to be the highest expression of human creativity; it can simply be whatever tickles man's pleasure in a certain culture and a certain historical epoch. If liturgy is no longer the worship of God but the cult of the self, it is understandable how sacred music no longer requires the aesthetic and ecstatic effort that demands long study and professionalism to guarantee a result that, albeit always inadequate to the divine majesty, would at least tend toward that perfection.

From the beginning of the 1980s, Joseph Ratzinger reflected at length on these points.[33] In his final work, published posthumously at his behest, one finds a brief discourse from 2015 titled "Music and Liturgy" (Benedetto XVI 2023, pp. 39–43) in which he recalls that, whereas in *Sacrosanctum Concilium* respect for sacred music and *participatio actuosa* were still "peacefully united," in the years immediately following Vatican II, a "dramatic tension" arose: the elimination of the patrimony of sacred music in favor of

[32] Innocent III, *De Sacro Altaris Mysterio*, III 6, PL vol. 217, col. 846; Robert Bellarmine, *De Missa*, I 2, 7.

[33] It is impossible to provide here a list of Ratzinger's writings on these subjects: this is a subject that has been developed in a range of his texts, from his lively essay *The Feast of Faith* to his mature *The Spirit of the Liturgy*. His attention to the meaning of sacred music within solid theological reflection is furthermore continuous throughout the thought of the great German theologian, evident in his autobiography (Ratzinger 1997b) and in his last work, *What Is Christianity? The Last Writings* (Benedetto XVI 2023). The eleventh volume of his *Opera Omnia* gathers his essays on the liturgy: 126 pages are dedicated to sacred music (Ratzinger 2010, pp. 573–698).

the continual and exclusive involvement of participants in the rite provoked "dismay at the cultural impoverishment which necessarily ensued." Ratzinger's response was essentially the same as that which we are proposing in this book: it is not possible to resolve the issue of sacred music without reflection on the true nature of music, in which we encounter the "totally other and totally great that arouses in man new modes of expression."

If theology places man in the center, the objective of music changes as well. A great theologian like Antonio Livi held that, today, the right order of things has been overturned. Whereas in the past dogma guided theology, which was performed in pastoral practice, today the order has been inverted: it is pastoral practice that guides theology, which then becomes almost dogmatic. The important principles, therefore, do not descend from God but arise from man.[34] This inversion has had devastating consequences, and not only for sacred music. The anthropological shift in theology still dominates theological discourse, deflecting this discipline from its true objective. Even the classic definition of the aim of liturgy (and of sacred music), namely the glory of God and the edification of the faithful, ought to suggest the precise and necessary order of things. The faithful cannot be ennobled and sanctified if God is not given the glory in the way that is proper and due. This has not been merely a development of recent decades: at the end of the nineteenth century and the beginning of the twentieth, Modernism saw in immanentism the proper vision of theology, and of liturgical theology in particular. St. Pius X, in his *Pascendi*, described the devastating contribution of immanentism thus:

[34] See Livi and Porfiri 2018.

> And thus, Venerable Brethren, the road is open for us to study the Modernists in the theological arena—a difficult task, yet one that may be disposed of briefly. The end to be attained is the conciliation of faith with science, always, however, saving the primacy of science over faith. In this branch the Modernist theologian avails himself of exactly the same principles which we have seen employed by the Modernist philosopher, and applies them to the believer: the principles of *immanence* and *symbolism*. The process is an extremely simple one. The philosopher has declared: *The principle of faith is immanent*; the believer has added: *This principle is God*; and the theologian draws the conclusion: *God is immanent in man*. Thus we have *theological immanence*. So too, the philosopher regards as certain that *the representations of the object of faith are merely symbolical*; the believer has affirmed that *the object of faith is God in Himself*; and the theologian proceeds to affirm that: *The representations of the divine reality are symbolical*. And thus we have *theological symbolism*. Truly enormous errors both, the pernicious character of which will be seen clearly from an examination of their consequences.[35]

Thus, all is reduced to subjectivism, to religious sentiment that naturally is a creation of man more than an emanation from God. In fact, Pius X continues:

[35] Pius X, *Pascendi Dominici Gregis* (1907), paragraph 19, https://www.vatican.va/content/pius-x/en/encyclicals/documents/hf_p-x_enc_19070908_pascendi-dominici-gregis.html.

> Religion, whether natural or supernatural, must, like every other fact, admit of some explanation. But when Natural theology has been destroyed, the road to revelation closed through the rejection of the arguments of credibility, and all external revelation absolutely denied, it is clear that this explanation will be sought in vain outside man himself. It must, therefore, be looked for in man; and since religion is a form of life, the explanation must certainly be found in the life of man. Hence the principle of *religious immanence* is formulated. Moreover, the first actuation, so to say, of every vital phenomenon, and religion, as has been said, belongs to this category, is due to a certain necessity or impulsion; but it has its origin, speaking more particularly of life, in a movement of the heart, which movement is called a *sentiment*. Therefore, since God is the object of religion, we must conclude that faith, which is the basis and the foundation of all religion, consists in a sentiment which originates from a need of the divine. This need of the divine, which is experienced only in special and favorable circumstances, cannot, of itself, appertain to the domain of consciousness; it is at first latent within the consciousness, or, to borrow a term from modern philosophy, in the *subconsciousness*, where also its roots lie hidden and undetected. (no. 7)

Therefore, the theological reasons that constitute the foundation of the crisis of sacred music proceed not from relatively recent circumstances but from a poisoned seed that first planted its roots much farther back in time—one might even detect them in the first traces of humanism that preceded the Renaissance. Not that we consider man's needs and aspirations to have no legitimate importance, but they miss the point of their existence when they are situated outside of the correct hierarchy of values. The religion of man is nothing other than self-celebration of a masturbatory sort, necessarily fruitless because, as Ratzinger emphasized on many occasions, it does not open man to otherness, but remains closed in the human horizon and thus can only be self-celebrating. And so, contemporary "sacred music" (which should not even be referred to in this manner) is only the logical consequence of the theological and doctrinal deviations that have afflicted the Church, and whose end is nowhere in sight.

2. The Cultural Reason

We cannot understand the reasons for the crisis of sacred music without identifying what have been the enormous cultural changes of the last centuries, changes that concern the way in which sacred music is structured as compared to profane music. Until the modern era, sacred music in the Catholic context constituted the center of attraction for creative and performative resources, especially in the Middle Ages. Our documentation on profane music shows that the linguistic structure of profane music (modality, rhythm, compositional techniques) was then tied to those of sacred music: consider for example the relationship between profane Middle French sequences, tropes, *prosulae*, and repertoire (troubadours and minstrels). Medieval sacred music was not in the least impermeable to what was happening outside the churches: consider the Italian *lauda* repertoire, which certainly received its impulse from popular music, although it assimilated it in a coherent and cohesive context.[36]

Although in the Renaissance this situation continued in large part, one begins to note there an emancipation of profane music from sacred music, which would become even more evident from the Baroque period onward. The birth and development of musical forms such as the lyrical opera, the concerto, the sonata, and so forth would give composers of profane music enormous possibilities, opening up new markets for musical talent. As regards sacred music and its relation to profane music, its apex would be reached in the eigtheenth and nineteenth centuries, when operatic language monopolized musical creativity, heavily influencing even the composition of liturgical music and sacred music in general, arousing (as seen in the previous chapter) the concerned reactions of Church documents from Leo XII onward. The twentieth century was a time of enormous technological and cultural changes, among them the commercialization of music through radio, television, cinema, CDs, digitalization, and so forth. These possibilities for commercializing music opened significant sources of revenue for musicians, with the consequent new resources of marketing for the sake of gaining ever larger markets. The entertainment multinationals, and, in more recent years, online distribution platforms, would not only force their own artists onto the market, but they would also create and manipulate the musical tastes of people through consumer propaganda and the capitalistic cult of novelty.

This reality, which in some countries is accompanied by the collapse of musical education, has allowed the attractiveness of

[36] It would be of no use to amass a bibliography here. We refer the reader to better-documented histories of music—e.g., to the classic volume of Cattin 1984 and, in the profane field, e.g., to Drumbl 1981 and Drumbl 2003. On the topic of *lauda* research is underway: see Gozzi 2010.

popular music, obviously immensely widespread, to touch even Catholic liturgy. Unfortunately, under the pretext of carrying out liturgical reform following Vatican II, this linguistic and artistic flattening found an opening to penetrate the temple of God. To understand why this happened, one must also consider the work in this sense of various new ecclesial movements that created new inventories of music for the liturgy (directly or indirectly), which heavily mimicked commercial music, and that also contributed to the perversion of the function of sacred music in the worship of God. In this sense, movements such as the Focolarini, the Renewal in the Spirit, and the Neocatechumenal Way come to mind (obviously, in this context, we are not criticizing the merits that these movements have had in other areas).

One of the most important moments of this change, a moment we could almost call symbolic, was that of the performance in Rome on April 27, 1966, of what would later be defined the "Beat Mass" or "Youth Mass." That was a truly important moment of rupture for a number of reasons: the fact that the Mass was celebrated in Rome, in the heart of the Catholic Church; the fact that it was celebrated in the Sala Borromini, belonging to the community of the Oratorian Fathers of Chiesa Nuova, previously active in the development of religious *lauda*; and the fact that this initiative involved important personalities of the Roman ecclesiastical world. The music for the celebration was composed by Marcello Giombini (1928–2003), an esteemed composer of scores for Westerns, horror films, and erotic films. Giombini, who certainly knew his trade as a score composer, by his own admission knew nothing about what he was being asked to do. This is how Alessandro Beltrami reports Giombini's declarations in *Avvenire* on March 3, 2016. The musician described his "sacred" opera in this manner:

> It was only a discographic phenomenon. I was not a man of the trade, I knew nothing about liturgy, even though I had liturgist friends who helped me. As a musician, however, I seemed to have discovered the need for religious song that was younger and closer to the way of life of those years, because in Church one heard only endless dirges. And so, I came up with a specific product like the Mass. Which in fact was quite successful, selling tens of thousands of copies.

Some might object to one fact: Great Renaissance composers like Orlando di Lasso composed remarkable sacred music, but also profane music that was decidedly licentious. Why should we be surprised by or indignant about Giombini? In reality, the situation is profoundly different due to the linguistic reasons recalled above: in the Renaissance, it was still sacred music that constituted the point of reference, and between the style of sacred music and that of profane music there existed an evident continuity. In this case, however, the music being proposed as "sacred" passively assumes the style of consumeristic music, and is destined to have a short life because it is tied to the fashions of the moment.

3. The Musical Reason

Speaking of cultural change, it was inevitable to highlight how changes in music also involved changes in culture. In fact, if we look more closely at music, we are forced to recognize how the crisis of sacred music has taken place at a moment of great crisis in musical language in what is often termed as "classical music." It is a crisis that has distanced many listeners from concert halls.

The refusal to consider the needs of the listener, coming up with compositions that lack any reference to tonal or modal structures, has created a gap between beneficiaries and performers that has inevitably left open ground for other musical genres, often of dubious quality, capable of attracting public attention, already oriented by the powers of modern marketing techniques. Commercial music has become for so many the only musical experience possible, being more user-friendly than, say, jazz. The situation is profoundly different with respect to the past: in the 1700s and 1800s, for example, music for consumption obviously existed, but fundamentally it employed the same language as "cultured" music, and therefore did not create otherness or ruptures but a substantial continuity. It suffices to consider the figures of great musicians like Schubert or Brahms. Unfortunately, a new sacred music has been forged in the linguistic setting of the lowest level of musical production, the most prosaic and lacking in artistic substance, that of commercial music.

Returning to sacred music strictly speaking, one cannot fail to observe how, after the Second Vatican Council, the mechanisms that could have guaranteed a continuity with the tradition of music in the liturgy were destroyed. Once composers, organists, cantors, and so forth were chased out of the churches, under the pretext that this service must be performed for free (an unfounded idea at odds with the Church's social teaching, which respects and promotes the value of work and professionality), the level of what was heard in the liturgy plummeted. If those who ought to guarantee the high artistic level of sacred music are eliminated, it cannot be expected to attain its true nature. It is sad to note that, in this matter, the responsibility of the Catholic Church herself is immense.

4. The Anthropological Reason

We have discussed previously the anthropological shift in theology. A particular variation of this shift, which concerns the crisis in sacred music as well, is that which expressed a certain desire to appear young. This was also fostered by the climate of the 1960s: the student protests, the diffusion of a new type of music that targeted kids, music that reflected a certain type of culture best encapsulated by the call to "tune in, turn on, and drop out." This moment is symbolized by Woodstock and by the French uprisings in May 1968. On the heels of the Second Vatican Council, it was thought that music influenced by the counterculture would bring youth back to church. At the distance of more than half a century, it must be recognized that this attempt, though certainly motivated by good intentions, ended in abysmal failure. The emptying out of churches, especially of youth, had its beginnings in this period. The desire to attract by falling into line with the dominant languages, with the going anthropology, rather than offering a proposal that was coherently demanding, constituted an error that is historically indisputable. The lack of discernment on the part of many pastors of that time seems evident; the result could only be the catastrophe before everyone's eyes (and in everyone's ears) today.

The most incisive analysis of this phenomenon of the desire to appear young and its bearing on the Catholic Church's strategy in those years was given by the Italian philosopher Roman Amerio in his magisterial *Iota Unum*. The following quotation is lengthy but is worth reading in its entirety:

> All the themes of the juvenilism of the contemporary world, in which the Church shares, come together in Pope Paul's speech to a group of hippies

who had come to Rome for a peace demonstration in April 1971. The Pope sketches and enumerates with praise those "secret values" young people are searching for.

The first is spontaneity, which doesn't strike the Pope as being at odds with searching, even though a sought spontaneity ceases to be spontaneous. Nor does spontaneity seem to him at odds with morality, even though the latter involves considered intentions, superimposes itself upon spontaneity, and can clash with it.

The second value is "liberation from certain formal and conventional ties." The Pope does not specify what they are. As for forms, they are the substance itself as it appears, that is as it enters the world. And as for conventions, they are what is agreed upon, that is they are consents, and are good things if they are consents to good things.

The third value is "the need to be themselves." But it is not made clear what self it is that the young person should realize and in which he should recognize his identity: there are in fact many selves in a free nature, which can be transformed into many guises. The true self does not demand that the young person realize himself any old how but that he be transformed and even become other than he is. The words of the Gospel, furthermore, will bear no gloss: abneget semetipsum. The day before, the Pope had been exhorting to metanoia. So then, is it realize yourself, or transform yourself?

> The fourth value is an enthusiasm "to live and interpret your own times." The Pope, however, offers the young people no interpretative key to their own times, since he does not point out that from the religious point of view, man must seek out the non-ephemeral among the ephemeral things of his own time, that is, seek out the last end that perdures through it all. Having thus developed his argument without any explicitly religious reference, Paul VI somewhat unexpectedly concludes by saying: "We think that in this interior search of yours you notice the need for God." The Pope is here certainly speaking speculatively rather than with his authority as teacher. (Amerio 1996, pp. 196–197)

Romano Amerio's analysis can be considered a most clear-minded vision of the slippage that was occurring already in the Magisterium of Paul VI in its stance toward the world. The Church seemed obliged now to esteem indiscriminately the values the world proposed, whether good or ill.

5. The Liturgical Reason

After Vatican II, the liturgy was reformed in a way very different from what was requested by the conciliar texts, which did not in the least call for a "new liturgy," one that would nevertheless be implemented in the years following the Council.[37] Despite the words of high esteem in *Sacrosanctum Concilium*, sacred music

[37] For historical documentation and bibliography, see, for example, Milanese 2005. Among the many reconstructions of the events of Vatican II, De Mattei 2019 with its attentive historical documentation should be noted.

went through a profound crisis immediately after Vatican II: beyond the reasons considered above, this was also due to the possibility that the new liturgy, elaborated in the second half of the 1960s, was to offer music. Above all, there is the issue of the length of the rites: today there is a preference for much more concise liturgies. Already in late antiquity, however, these problems were not absent: Caesarius of Arles roused his flock on several occasions to patient attention in the sixth century. But the situation of continuous "noise," and the communicative siege in which contemporary humanity lives, has created a situation without precedent. One must not habituate oneself to the dominant anthropological situation: "The Church must remain demanding" (Ratzinger 2010, p. 601). The Church must educate people in the rhythm of the liturgy and the important part that true sacred music has in it, as will be discussed below.

There is also a question that overlapped with the liturgical reform, and which a Servite liturgist, Fr. Silvano Maggiani (who died recently), termed "participationism." This idea states that everyone must "do" something in the liturgy: read, sing, gesture, dance. Why should participation be understood only as emitting sounds (speaking or singing) and not receiving sounds (listening, meditating). For example, must one who has difficulty in singing be forced to do so? There exist various forms of participation, and listening is not the lesser of them. According to this mentality, the choir is stealing something that belongs to everyone: singing. Obviously, it is an entirely erroneous idea, because the choir sings in the name of the assembly insofar as it is capable of offering praise to God in song in a more worthy manner. Some say that God is not concerned with the way in which we sing and that He accepts even singing that is out of tune. The truth is that God accepts that singing by one who cannot do otherwise. But is it a sign of respect toward God's majesty to offer cacophonous singing when it could be done much better? The result of such a leveling down is very dangerous.

Another result of this limiting conception of participation as "doing" is verbosity: the liturgy has been padded with discourses and various considerations on the part of not a few priests. The theologian Roberto Tagliaferri in his book *The Broken Cup* observes:

> Liturgical practice suffers this mental deformation that thinks that verbal content is more powerful and original than scenic perceptions. This deformation sees as a cruelty to the liturgy the urgent necessity of a return to the stage, in other words the aesthetic languages of music, of celebration, of dance, of costume, of perfume, etc. This entire setting has been liquidated by the cultivators of the conciliar reform, expunging the ghost of ritualism, confusing the epistemological problematic of the languages of the Sacred with the juridical and clerical drift of post-Tridentine rubricism. The anti-performative conditioning of the post-Conciliar period has led the Church to invoke a full secularization of the rite in favor of verbal and psychological-moral languages, as a pre-condition for access to the *veritas* of the Christian sacrament. After the Council, the Italian Church inaugurated an evangelization style that would save the sacraments from their formality because by themselves they offered insufficient guarantees of total belonging to the explicit Creed of the Church.

> According to this vision, only those who believe and know the doctrine of the mysteries through catechesis can take part fruitfully in the Christian liturgy. Not the least suspicion that there might be a more complex linguistic level to faith than the explicit word!

6. The Pedagogical Reason

Here we must confront a topic that obviously has many ramifications: the Church has renounced her role as educator of the faithful. Once upon a time, the Church formed people's tastes through her art, music, and spirituality. In this manner, she was one of the motors of our civilization. Then she seems to have renounced this role to chase after the trends of the moment. This has most certainly been the reason for the loss of the sense of catholicity in art and music, which have often become the tools of secular phenomena. In the past, education concerned all levels of society, from children to the elderly. Today, many of the pedagogical instruments the Church proposes are loaded with sociological and psychological influences and lack the indispensable link with the doctrinal and spiritual spheres.

7. The Sociological Reason

In the last century, the push to renounce the concept of the sacred was quite strong, and so too was the concept of authority, which rests on a hierarchical and sacral vision of life and the universe. Only by recognizing that legitimate authority comes from God, and therefore has a sacred character, can we give order to our existence. The concept of authority has been the object of intense contestation, not only directed at individual authority figures but also as concerns what, or who, is authoritative, even in the arts. In the setting of sacred music, this has been expressed in an upheaval of perspective with respect to the Liturgical Movement. At its beginnings, in the case of Pius X, Gregorian chant and classic polyphony were indicated as the models to follow, as far as sacred music was concerned. In the post-conciliar period, despite *Sacrosanctum Concilium*, these repertoires became cumbersome burdens to be jettisoned, and no equally valid and effective substitute was put in place. The "noble simplicity" of which *Sacrosanctum Concilium* speaks (no. 34) has become irrelevant: "A simple matter is not identical to economical or cheap. There exists the simplicity of the prosaic and there exists the simplicity which is the expression of maturity" (Ratzinger 2010, p. 599).

The Question of Latin and Gregorian Chant

1. Latin and Liturgy

AMONG THE FAVORITE targets of those who pushed for a radical reform of Catholic liturgy is the Latin language and Gregorian chant. In reality, this common consideration should not surprise us: on the contrary, it is perfectly logical when one comprehends that Latin and Gregorian chant are intimately united. Some will mention the fact that there have been many attempts to translate Gregorian chant into various vernacular languages, and we shall return to this later.

We said previously that according to the intentions of the pope who convened and opened the Second Vatican Council, John XXIII, the use of Latin in the liturgy and in the life of the Church was not in question. In fact, he even recommended its use in the document cited in the previous chapter, *Veterum Sapientia*, an apostolic constitution (theoretically still in force) that presents considerations of great refinement regarding the relationship between the Church and the Latin language. Roncalli highlighted the capacity of Latin to avoid creating situations of privilege for the speakers of one language with respect to others, placing everyone in the condition of equality. This consideration is particularly shrewd in light of the current prevalence of a sort of "global English," as the use of English as the lingua franca obtains the effect of privileging the native speakers of this language, whereas the papal document observes that Latin is egalitarian and favors no people over another. In this document, nothing is said of liturgical Latin, which was still considered an uncontestable fact.

Not even two years after Roncalli's *Veterum Sapientia*, Latin was the object of intense debate within the Council itself, but in the final deliberations over the liturgy, contained in *Sacrosanctum Concilium*, they continued to describe as normal the use of this language for the Roman Rite: in fact, it was stated, *Linguae latinae usus, salvo particulari iure, in Ritibus latinis servetur* (no. 36). The Latin language in the Roman Rite had to be preserved, except for particular exceptions in special traditions in which other languages were used. The very word, *servetur*, was used with respect to the patrimony of sacred music: *Thesaurus Musicae sacrae summa cura servetur et foveatur*. Here we learn that the patrimony of sacred music must be not only preserved but also sustained and made to flourish.[38] One must observe that the standard to be preserved and fostered is the patrimony of sacred music, not just any music to be used in the liturgy: in other words, repertoires such as Gregorian chant and polyphony, which have represented it, even in magisterial pronouncements, were the models to be followed. How we arrived at the current state of affairs is not easy to understand. The current state of the matter is certainly an unprecedented rupture with the tradition of the Church and the documents of Vatican II, if these documents are read for what they effectively say, without superimposing on them an arbitrary interpretive framework.

One might ask: *Why should Latin have been preserved?* The question is asked in the past tense because, despite the fact that Latin was never abolished for liturgical use, today it is extremely rare in our celebrations of the Mass of Paul VI, the Mass

[38] The verb employed here, *foveo*, recurs often in this text, always with the meaning of "to favor, to foster, to promote," from the very first article in which it is found twice in as many lines.

celebrated with the current missal, although it could be celebrated in Latin. Latin is in fact employed almost exclusively by those who celebrate with the pre-conciliar missal, which has led to the erroneous equation according to which the use of Latin coincides with the use of the pre-conciliar missal: quite often one reads expressions such as "Latin Mass" as an equivalent to "antiquated Mass." The error is obvious, but one can see the reason for it, given that just a few years after the close of Vatican II, before the publication of the present Mass, the liturgical books were already widely translated into national languages, with the exception of the Canon of the Mass (see, for example, the English–Latin Roman Missal, approved in 1965 and published in 1966). This bogus equivalence, along with the erroneous view that the current missal was willed by Vatican II, has led many to consider the use of Latin as a "pre-conciliar" choice and thus implicitly "anti-conciliar," an entirely unfounded affirmation, albeit a widely held one.

Many authoritative participants at Vatican II were convinced that the affirmations of the Council would have been taken seriously. Cardinal Giuseppe Siri (1906–1989), archbishop of Genoa and one of the most notable churchmen of the day, a man who always sought to maintain a balanced position during those difficult years, affirmed in a pastoral letter in 1965:

> You will hear parts of the Holy Mass recited in Italian or connected rites which previously you understood in Latin; you will notice some slight modifications or innovations which will be explained in good time. The fixed parts of the solemn Mass will continue to be sung in a Latin that is by now familiar to so many of us. Beyond

> these innovations, made for your benefit, the sacred ministers will continue to use Latin in the Divine Office and in the sacred rites. The old marvelous language will not disappear in the least, and just as it bound together two thousand years of culture and forged unity in Europe, it will continue to offer its assistance to the unity of the Church. (Siri 1978, pp. 119–120)

Siri's text follows to the letter the work of *Sacrosanctum Concilium*: even when he asserts "the sacred ministers will continue to use Latin in the Divine Office," the cardinal quotes implicitly the conciliar text (no. 101: clerics must celebrate the Office in Latin, a disposition repeated in other documents promulgated immediately after Vatican II, which all confirm the necessity of a serious teaching of Latin in seminaries).

Another episode from that same year reiterates the close link between Latin, sacred music, and the poor application of the actual decrees of Vatican II. Pope Paul VI in person reassured the worried president of the Pontifical Institute of Sacred Music, Msgr. Higini Anglès, about the future of sacred music in the liturgy of the Church. Anglès wrote to Fr. Laurence Feininger, the great American musicologist and musician who carried out most of his work in Trent, reassuring him of the situation. Feininger intuited that the future was bleak and that a collapse of sacred music and the liturgy was on the horizon. Anglès also said that the reform movement of liturgical music appeared "directed by people illiterate in the field of sacred music," but declared nonetheless his moderate optimism after his meeting with Montini:

> Yesterday, I finally had the good fortune of having a private audience with the Holy Father. We spoke a lot about this subject that is so close to our hearts. He was the one who promised me that everything would change and that the musical patrimony of the Church would be once more held in honor.[39]

The situation rapidly headed in another direction, as Feininger had soberly feared, and for the rest of his life he refused to celebrate the new Mass, showing in his person the close relationship between Latin and sacred music. The decrees of the Holy See in that period continued to refer to the texts of Vatican II: in addition to recalling the obligation to learn Latin in priestly formation, Paul VI published the instruction *Musicam Sacram* in 1967, in which he defended the use of Gregorian chant and the musical tradition. By that point, the practice of celebrating in national languages had already spread so widely that the document indicated the necessity of maintaining at least in some churches the use of Latin in the liturgy (no. 48). The situation, then, was getting out of control: already in 1965, Paul VI had expressed his dismay. Consider the encyclical *Mysterium Fidei*, in which he observed that, as concerns the meaning of the Mass, there had arisen "no small measure of confusion about matters of faith, just as if it were all right for someone to take doctrine that has already been defined by the Church and consign it to oblivion" (no. 10). The confusion cited by Montini reflected necessarily on the considerations on sacred music.

An English scholar, Michael Davies, published a booklet in which he asserted that "time bombs" were planted in the texts of

[39] The quote was taken from the Archive Curti-Feininger. See Calliari 2022, p. 152.

Vatican II, phrases that, taken out of context, could lead one to declare as "conciliar" affirmations that in reality did not completely correspond to the texts (Davies 2003). Davies's exegetical approach is at times quite rigid, as in his other publications, but is essentially correct: conciliar documents frequently establish a line of principle, and then add "exceptional" possibilities or special concessions that, taken out of context, are employed in creating new practices. The case of the Divine Office, to be sung or read in Latin, except for individual exceptional cases, is significant: the "individual cases" for "serious impediments" foreseen by *Sacrosanctum Concilium* became, already just four years later in *Musicam Sacram* in 1967, so normalized that they were regulated in some way (no. 41), prescribing the composition of new melodies for those who sing the Divine Office in the local national languages. Thus, in four years, the exceptional "serious impediments" had become the rule.

Joseph Ratzinger often observed, even in the years long before his ascension to the papal throne, that a sort of "parallel truth" had been created by which one attributed to Vatican II decisions that were completely absent from the Council texts, as in the case of abolishing Latin.[40] In most seminaries today, Latin (the language that is still the Church's official language) is no longer taught. The documents of Vatican II and of Paul VI have been erased from the collective historical memory and a new narrative has been created, a falsifying one founded on exceptions (the "nevertheless" and the "but also" in the key reference texts) that have led to the hermeneutical discontinuity that Benedict XVI spoke out against.

[40] See, for example, Cardinal Ratzinger's preface to *Conversi ad Dominum* by U.M. Lang, p. 7.

2. Latin in the History of the Liturgy

The most frequent objection advanced against the use of Latin in the liturgy is that it renders the participation of the faithful impossible because the vast majority do not understand it. This issue has already been discussed in the previous chapter, and we can benefit from reconsidering the piercing observations of Ratzinger, returning for a moment to the problem, given its central importance to the use of Latin and Gregorian chant. As Ratzinger emphasizes, we must not smooth over the concept of participation as always needing to "do" something: listening is also participation. And, in the case of comprehension of the liturgical text, it must be remembered that the Mass is not a meeting or a conference: the Mass is founded on being admitted into the presence of something that transcends and thus is not a continuation of daily life, but rather enters into the supernatural. The concept of "comprehension," which we have been led to conceive of as only verbal, takes on an entirely different meaning. It is truly *cum prehendere*, literally *taking together*. It is not limited to "understanding" the meaning of certain words, which at times becomes so central and exclusive that it leads to verbalism. In that moment, we must assume the attitude of St. Thomas Aquinas before his death, who in the face of the vision of God understood how fragile everything he had written really was (and this was St. Thomas Aquinas!).

We must never forget that the classic definition of the purpose of the liturgy, "for the glory of God and the edification of the faithful," must be read and perceived in that order. Only if we are capable of giving adequate glory to God can we "edify ourselves"—in other words, build ourselves up interiorly. It is not our personal edification that gives glory to God: God does not need us, but we need God. The liturgy is by its nature always vertical, not horizontal: it is not resolved in conversation among those present, but in their opening toward a different dimension. We are called to *discover the other universe*, to use the phrase of Theodossios Sgourdelis. In this context, the use of a language that is especially employed for liturgical use, as is the case in almost every traditional religion, acquires all the necessary meaning. In this horizon, the concept of sacred language must be understood. This concept is not exclusive to Christianity (which, besides Latin, makes use of Byzantine Greek, for example, Church Slavonic, and Syriac). Consider, beyond the Christian world, biblical Hebrew, or Quranic Arabic.[41]

The following argument underlies the devaluation of Latin:

1. The liturgy was originally in Greek.
2. To make comprehension of the liturgy possible, it passed into Latin, which was in late antiquity the language of the common people.
3. Therefore, the same move must be made today, and we must move away from Latin to vernacular languages.

This argument is in reality profoundly mistaken. Around the mid-twentieth century, a group of researchers at the Dutch Catholic University dedicated themselves to the study of the origins of Christian Latin. Although the conclusions of these scholars were at least in part corrected by later research (see the recent historical

[41] The treatment of the concept of sacred language in the second chapter of U. M. Lang's *The Voice of the Church at Prayer* offers a helpful clarification, as does the fourth chapter of his book *The Roman Mass*. Roberto De Mattei's *Latin in the Life of the Church* is also useful, as are the rich observations of Amerio in his *Iota Unum*.

study of Denecker 2018), the framework laid down by Christine Mohrmann regarding the origins of liturgical Latin remains absolutely solid. The origins of Christian preaching in the western Mediterranean are tied to Greek: St. Paul was culturally both Greek and Hebrew, and from the Acts of the Apostles we can see clearly his ability to pass from Greek to Aramaic (the Greek text says "Hebrew," but the language spoken at the time among Jews was Aramaic).[42] The extended use of Greek as the liturgical language even in the West can be easily explained by the fact that Greek had for centuries already developed a biblical lexicon: the Greek Septuagint had already been in circulation at the time of early Christian preaching for about three centuries and was esteemed even by pagan intellectuals, such as the ancient literary critic Longinus. The Bible had not yet been translated into Latin, and therefore a vocabulary suitable for conveying the concepts of nascent Christianity was completely lacking. The Bible was eventually translated into Latin, and only afterward was it possible to turn Latin into a liturgical language. Around the second century the first Latin translations of the Bible came into existence, and writers like Tertullian already displayed an elaborate Latin vocabulary for discussing theology. The use of Latin in the liturgy must have followed the translations of the Bible into Latin. As had happened centuries earlier with Greek, the translation of the Bible provided the lexical and linguistic terrain on which the liturgical texts could be constructed. The chronology frequently proposed, which suggests that Latin was introduced in the liturgy when the faithful were no longer capable of understanding Greek, is decidedly simplistic. Latin must have been admitted into the liturgy proper (prayers, altar texts, hymns) in a second moment,

[42] On Greek and the Greeks in the New Testament, see Windisch 1967.

and probably slowly, not only due to the naturally conservative quality of any liturgical language, but because the language of any serious liturgy needs a very mature period of "general" language: Christian liturgy required a technical language already rooted in the minds of the clergy and the faithful, capable of reaching a sufficiently elevated level without sacrificing intelligibility.

After the end of the persecutions in the fourth century, as Christine Mohrmann observed, the new status of Christianity in Roman society had made possible the use of "pagan" words that previously had been considered inappropriate to Christian vocabulary: for example, the neologism *salvator*, to translate the Greek σωτήρ (sotér), began to be used in the second century as a typically Christian word instead of the classical Latin *conservator*, which was too bound to pagan meanings.[43] But this latter word was later accepted by Christian writers who could allow themselves to reutilize the learned pagan vocabulary from which earlier Christian centuries sought to distance themselves to highlight the novelty of the Christian message. In essence, the now stable situation of Christianity in society made it possible to develop a Christian language that no longer feared absorbing elements of "pagan" Latin. In this linguistic and cultural context liturgical Latin was born, and it was stylistically and lexically already quite mature: two hundred years had passed since the first Latin translations of the Bible, and the Latin of the Christians had by now become a language that was perfectly capable of serving the needs of the liturgy. It must also be added, as Mohrmann observed on several occasions, that the liturgical

[43] In the Vulgate (the translation of the Bible revised by St. Jerome) the word *conservator* never appears, while the neologism *salvator* appears ninety-eight times.

language has a naturally conservative tendency, and that this element also led (albeit slowly) to the adoption of liturgical Latin.[44] The style, the language, and the vocabulary of liturgical Latin (e.g., the Canon of the Mass) display a high level of composition and do not correspond at all to a language merely on the level of common usage: it was not a Latin introduced for reasons of mundane comprehensibility, but because the language had reached the necessary maturity.[45]

U.M. Lang synthesizes with habitual clarity this historical data in his recent volume on the history of the Mass (Lang 2022, pp. 109–110), and in a more didactic manner in his intervention at a convention in 2008 on the *motu proprio Summorum Pontificum*:

> The development of a Latin liturgy was not a simple adoption of the "vernacular" language in the liturgy, given that the Latin of the Roman Canon, the Collects, and the Prefaces of the Mass, was detached from the idiom of the common people. It was a heavily stylized language that the average Christian in Rome of late antiquity would have had difficulty understanding, especially considering the fact that the level of education was quite low with respect to our times. Furthermore, the development of *latinitas Christiana* might have made the liturgy more accessible to the people of Rome or

44 Mohrmann's studies on liturgical Latin and its formation are quite numerous. Some of her main works in this field are gathered in the volume *Latin chrétien et liturgique*.

45 On the Canon of the Mass see the interesting works Botte 1935 and Mohrmann 1965, pp. 227–244; in general, on the Ordinary of the Mass, the locus classicus remains Botte and Mohrmann 1953.

> Milan, but not necessarily to those whose native language was Gothic, Celtic, Iberic, or Punic. It is possible to imagine a Western Church with local languages in its liturgy, like in the East, where in addition to Greek, they used Syriac, Coptic, Armenian, Georgian, and Ethiopian. In any case, the situation in the West was fundamentally different; the unifying force of the papacy was such that Latin had become the sole liturgical language. This was an important factor in fostering ecclesiastical, cultural and political cohesion. *Latinitas* became one of the foundations of Christendom.[46]

What the simplistic reconstructions sustain is therefore historically unfounded. Christine Mohrmann herself summarized the question with great lucidity in one of her conferences held in Washington:

> Liturgical Latin, as constituted towards the end of Christian Antiquity and preserved unchanged—in its main lines at least—down to the present time, is a deliberately sacral stylization of Early Christian Latin as it gradually developed in the Christian communities of the West. The Latin Christians were comparatively late in creating a liturgical language. When they did so, the Christian idiom had already reached full maturity and circumstances rendered it possible (for stylistic purposes) to draw on the ancient sacral heritage of Rome. This would have been

46 The text is available online on various sites, for example: http://www.internetica.it/Lang-LatinoLinguaLiturgica.htm.

> impossible during the first centuries, given the original repugnance to anything connected with paganism.... I think ... that we are justified in asking whether, at the present time, the introduction of the vernacular into the liturgy would not mean more loss than gain. First and foremost, there is the question, which, as we have seen, also troubled the first centuries, whether or not the vernacular would be suitable for the composition of a sacral prayer style.... Modern, so-called Western languages are ... less suitable for sacred stylization. And yet we must realize that sacral stylization forms an essential element of every official prayer language and that this sacral, hieratic character cannot, and should never, be relinquished. From the point of view of the general development of the Western languages—to say nothing of the problems raised by other languages—the present time is certainly not propitious for the abandonment of Latin. (Mohrmann 1957, pp. 83–86)

To summarize these considerations, we can conclude with the following:

- ✠ The use of a sacred language destined for liturgical worship is a common fact of religious experience.
- ✠ The affirmation that posits a parallelism between the actual elimination of Latin in the past fifty years and the introduction of Latin in the fourth century is unfounded.

Furthermore, it must be observed that the use of Latin in the liturgy for more than fifteen centuries cannot, from the historical point of view, be eliminated in a sudden manner. It took Latin three centuries to become a language suited to the liturgy. This use was so profoundly sedimented into the life of the Church that to relinquish it from one moment to the next could only bring about the turmoil we are now witnessing. Was there no reflection on the fact that so many centuries could not be erased from one moment to another? The issue is even stranger because it was carried out in a time in which the possibilities offered by technology and progress in means of communication actually highly favored those who wished to understand all that was said and sung during the Mass. Not only were the missalettes with the original texts and the translations of use, but there are other resources today that have enriched the pedagogical methods, and which could allow for a verbal comprehension of the texts, beginning with the rich offering provided by the Internet.

Examined in their entirety, then, the positions of those who condemn the use of Latin are either falsifying (in the case of those attributing to Vatican II a desire for the elimination of Latin) or lacking in historical foundation.

3. Gregorian Chant and the Liturgy

Gregorian chant is intimately bound to the Latin language, and therefore consideration of it could only be made after having examined the problem of liturgical Latin. There were in fact many attempts to translate Gregorian chant into the vernacular languages, but they were attempts destined to fail because this song is so intimately bound to the Latin language that these translations ended up deprived of meaning. In the case of the vernacular languages, it is much better to propose new compositions than to use the stylistic structures of Gregorian chant and its modal and rhythmic approach, because the music can be shaped directly on the text in the vulgate with results that are definitely more appreciated. The link between Gregorian chant and Latin is also quite tight on the phonetic level as well: Gregorian composition uses structures based on the position of the Latin accent, and Latin pronunciation is an essential element.[47]

But why be so concerned about Gregorian chant? In reality, it is the Church herself that has always venerated this repertoire, to the point of recognizing it (a unique case) as its own genre of song: "The Church acknowledges Gregorian chant as especially suited to the Roman liturgy" (*Sacrosanctum Concilium*, no. 116). Its importance is not only as an artistic treasure but above all as witness to an experience of profound prayer and meditation: Gregorian chant is theology and exegesis in musical form. The Church cultivated it not for aesthetic purposes but for ecstatic purposes. She understood that Gregorian chant could represent a valid path of prayer, and as such it was a means she offered to all the faithful. But today, Gregorian chant has been swept out of our churches. What have we gained in exchange? I believe the response is so sad that it would be painful to utter.

Naturally, reasons were found for justifying the fact that Gregorian chant, despite the dispositions of Vatican II asking to preserve it in the liturgy, were *de facto* expelled from it. One of these reasons recalls once again the concept of participation so often referred to: the concept of participation connected merely to "doing something" at all costs, in this case singing. So, if people do not sing, they say, it means they are not participating. It would be like saying that we do not participate during the homily, because we are not speaking (indeed, from this unhealthy idea was

47 See the data produced by Milanese 2014 and Milanese 2015, with a bibliography of previous studies.

born the so-called "dialogue homily"). In this case as well, the Second Vatican Council says none of the things that these radical liturgists would like it to say:

> With zeal and patience, pastors of souls must promote the liturgical instruction of the faithful, and also their active participation in the liturgy both internally and externally, taking into account their age and condition, their way of life, and standard of religious culture. By so doing, pastors will be fulfilling one of the chief duties of a faithful dispenser of the mysteries of God; and in this matter they must lead their flock not only in word but also by example. (*Sacrosanctum Concilium*, no. 19)

Participation, therefore, is not only exterior but also interior (*participationem internam et externam*, as the Latin text says). Listening is also participation, and listening to profoundly spiritual music like Gregorian chant will certainly help to elevate the faithful to God.

Another excuse is that Gregorian chant must make room for "today's music." It is certainly to be welcomed that sacred music be enriched with new compositions, but one must scrutinize what "today's music" might mean. For some this idea means commercial music, which is today's music in the same way that pornography is today's cinema. Should we show the latter in our parish halls? One must be very prudent when playing with words. There are also important composers of good sacred music in our day, both in the Catholic world and among the Protestant churches. Why should one necessarily fall into line with commercial music? The fact of its vast diffusion does not mean that it is appropriate for divine worship. Pornography is also very widespread, as are drug use and marital separation. Not all that is pervasive must be considered good *in se*.

Furthermore, Gregorian chant does not impede the production of new repertoires: to the contrary, familiarity with the foundational repertoire of Gregorian chant is a precondition for which composers of new music can truly possess a compositional ability to confer to their works the liturgical quality that allows them to be used in divine worship. This was already affirmed by St. Pius X in 1903 and is a rule that is certainly valid today. The model of Gregorian chant allows for true innovation, the true "music of today," if we wish to maintain this definition. Unfortunately, the hasty removal of this great patrimony has obtained the result of liturgical and musical desolation in our churches. Moreover, the so-called "music of today" introduced into the liturgy has not had the desired result of bringing people to church—churches are emptier than ever.

A further reason adopted for justifying the expulsion of Gregorian chant and the great musical tradition from churches is that we no longer have the musical forces to execute such a repertoire. This is one of my favorite arguments, because it truly shows how the text we quoted from Confucius with respect to rectifying names reveals a profound truth. Why are there no more performers capable of executing this repertoire? Simply because they were expelled from the churches: people capable of performing this demanding work are out there, but they are not permitted to do their work. And this is not merely a problem with devaluing the idea of musical professionalism, such that those who are musicians in church with an adequate preparation are adequately recompensed, just like the sacristan is recompensed, or the florist, or the electrician; but also, when these musicians perform freely as volunteers, they often run up against ideological hostility. A well-prepared musician is justified in refusing to play or sing repertoires of an unacceptable sort, instead directing their professional attention to music performed outside of churches. No doubt, the issue of compensation for church musicians is more important in some countries than in others: in the United States, England, or Germany, there still exist favorable conditions, at least in some cases, for church musicians. But especially in countries with ancient Catholic traditions like Italy, Spain, and Portugal, the situation is not so rosy. Perhaps France is still an exception, to some extent. In Italy, however, there has been a deliberate quest to eradicate musical professionalism by all means available, and still the work of destruction has not finished. The means are there, but unfortunately, one no longer invests in this field, and as a consequence we see the free fall in the quality of sacred music. It is also true that fewer people attend church, and thus there are fewer resources to go around. But someone must pose the question: If after decades of reforms this is the result, were these reforms really what the faithful needed? Do we not realize that the problem was certainly not to be found in Gregorian chant?

Some maintain that Gregorian chant could be done away with because it is boring or "a drag." That Gregorian chant can be performed in a tedious manner is indeed true. But the same can be said of any other repertoire, including the light music, often saccharine and trite, in use in many churches today. Gregorian chant, when properly executed, is celestial music that truly facilitates and aids prayer. But as for all repertoires, it must be performed appropriately. Therefore, it is not Gregorian chant that is tedious but certain executions of it that have made it seem so.

Whereas research in recent decades has demonstrated that Gregorian chant is extremely varied and quite rich from the rhythmic and modal point of view, an erroneous divulgation that has dominated for nearly half a century has transformed Gregorian chant into a series of notes all of equal duration, resulting in a general leveling and the disappearance of the rich compositional variety mentioned.[48] This forced "egalitarianism," *in se* destructive of the musicality of Gregorian chant, is often accompanied by an execution that is almost uniformly *sotto voce*, certainly anti-musical, and at times soporiferous (at odds with the ancient manuscripts, which used the indication *klangor*, or "sing loudly"). This is not Gregorian chant but rather a distortion of it by certain parties.

Gregorian chant should also be promoted for its interreligious and potentially ecumenical value. This might sound odd, but it ought to be considered attentively. The musical language of Gregorian chant is related to many other compositional traditions. For example, the structure of many introits (hymns performed at the beginning of Mass) is similar to the compositional structure of songs from Maghrebi Africa, the *maqam*. This should not surprise us in the least given the Mediterranean origins, in part, of Gregorian chant (Antonelli 1988). From the

[48] We can only mention this problem in passing here: the forced dissemination of Gregorian chant is one of the negative effects of its rediscovery at the end of the nineteenth and beginning of the twentieth centuries. The wide dissemination method has never been applied, moreover, in the very setting in which the idea was born, the French Abbey of Solesmes, as the former director of the abbey choir testified (see Claire 1990). It was a monk of Solesmes who began modern research into Gregorian chant, rediscovering its richness (see Cardine 1979). This text, originally published in French (Cardine 1970), has been translated into many languages, from Spanish to English to Japanese.

modal point of view, Gregorian can be compared with eastern Mediterranean musical traditions, and even with music from the Far East. In fact, some pieces present a pentatonic structure: this is the case, for example, in the communion hymn for Christmas Eve, "In Splendoribus," constructed on a clear pentatonic base. Pentatonic structures characterize many musical traditions, such as the classical Chinese tradition. There has been much research in this field, from the classic book on the relation between Christian music and synagogue music (Werner 1959), to the ethno-musicological research of Marius Schneider (Schneider 1962; Schneider 1999), to studies on modality by Jean Claire, Alberto Turco, and their students and collaborators. Gregorian chant, in other words, constitutes a pillar of Western music despite being open to contact with other worlds. This element could serve as a point of mutual understanding and solid union with other religious traditions compared, unlike the musical rubbish we hear in the liturgy today (see Kurkdjian 2016).

Sacred Music and Contemporary Culture

IN THE PRECEDING chapters, we confronted questions of great importance concerning the relationship between sacred music and the times in which we are living. We must now consider this matter in greater detail. In reality, the relationship between the Catholic Church and contemporary culture is a central theme we can use to read the great crisis of faith in which we are immersed.

To be sure we have a sharp focus on the scope of the problems facing us, we must once more confide in the wisdom of Confucius and "rectify names." At times, in fact, terms are used that take for granted that the object of discourse is clear to everyone, while in reality, insidious misunderstandings hide under an apparent simplicity of language.

For example, when important churchmen use the word *culture*, it seems they take for granted that everyone agrees on the meaning of that word. But is that really the case? What is culture? Upon reflection, the question is much more complex than we might think.[49] The term derives from the Latin *colere*, which means "to cultivate." It is related to *cultus*, worship.[50]

[49] We thank Vania Russo, Roberto Pecchioli, and Giacomo Maria Prati for having read the first draft of these paragraphs on the concept of culture and giving useful suggestions to improving the text.

[50] One must give due attention to the translation of *cultus* in Italian and in other languages. Although the translation is quite similar to Latin in the Italian, English, and French words, the meaning changes significantly. In Italian, the word *culto* is quite neutral and usually has a positive connotation, while in English *cult* and in French *culte* it can have both a positive and a negative meaning. The *Oxford English*

It seems that the first modern scholar to provide a definition of this term was Edward Burnett Tylor, an English anthropologist of the late nineteenth century. In his two-volume work *Primitive Culture,* he articulated for the first time the modern concept of culture. How did Tylor introduce this concept in his book? He wrote: "Culture or civilization, taken in its wide ethnographic sense, is that complex whole which includes knowledge, belief, art, morals, law, custom, and any other capabilities and habits acquired by man as a member of society."

It is interesting to linger on Tylor's emphasis of culture as that "complex whole." It is actually quite difficult to speak of this term univocally, as is often done when used in an instrumental sense. At times one confuses, willingly perhaps, culture with subcultures, those particular expressions of some groups, however extensive, that do not belong to the whole of social life. For example, many Italians belong to the subculture of comic-book readers, though not all Italians do. It is not a constitutive element of the broader culture of the Italian people, as is, for example, the Italian language. Furthermore, it is useful to reflect on the fact that this system, precisely because of its complexity, is also strongly constitutive of a robust, specific identity. It becomes a sign of fidelity that extends through time and space. Its complexity derives also from cultural elaborations that are closely tied to identity, and which we see threatened today by

Dictionary's second meaning for the word *cult* is "A relatively small group of people having (esp. religious) beliefs or practices regarded by others as strange or sinister, or as exercising excessive control over members." In Italian, a negative value appears only, for example, in expressions such as "cult of personality." The etymology of *culture* and *cultus* from the verb *colo* was well known to the ancients as well.

mass media through simplifications and the manipulation of words and history, which give life to perverse phenomena such as cancel culture and wokeness.

Is it necessary to speak of culture or cultures? In this sense, it is very dangerous that the clergy, who should have a catholic (in its original sense of *universal*) vision, speak of culture as if it were a single phenomenon, although it is obvious they should be addressing cultures. Here too we must be careful not to relativize everything, as if every culture were to be accepted uncritically. This is not a positive attitude. As in other fields, the recommendations of Vatican II concerning dialogue with the various cultures of the world have been interpreted poorly, transforming dialogue with cultures into a simple acceptance of their ideas.

As regards the relationships between cultures, liturgy, and music specifically, Joseph Ratzinger wrote on this in his *Spirit of the Liturgy*. He asked, in effect, which culture the Catholic Church must address. The answer is quite simple, it seems: *she must address her own culture*. Inculturation is primarily carried out by "developing a Christian culture in all of its various dimensions" (Ratzinger 2001, p. 197). Once, the Church was the promoter of her own culture, which was incarnated in Catholic theology, Catholic thought, Catholic art, Catholic music, and a Catholic vision of the world. Having lost this Catholic vision of things, and having therefore lost a culture that could be called *Catholic*, people began to chase after the cultural tendencies of the moment without the necessary critical view and without the capacity to discern what is good from what is not. This was a failure with catastrophic consequences.

The regression of the Church from the cultural field, whatever the meaning one wishes to give this word, was a tragedy whose effects we are still witnessing today. This is not a matter of rejecting contemporary culture, of which we shall speak in a moment. The Church has always been in step with the times, possessing the necessary capacity to sift through the cultural offerings of the various periods, to keep what is not good from penetrating her sacred precincts. On this issue, one can cite the thought of the important American intellectual John Senior, who at the end of the twentieth century, after having diagnosed the death of Christian culture, saw the hopes of a recovery in new pedagogical practices.

Analogously, Ratzinger observed that culture "is above all education, understanding this word in its most profound sense as an interior opening of man to his possibilities, in which he can develop even his exterior potential in conformity with his talents" (Ratzinger 2001, p. 197). Enrico Berti, one of the greatest scholars on Christian antiquity, has shown that the discourse of St. Paul to the Athenians must be interpreted as the first moment of intercultural relations between the biblical and classical traditions (Berti 2020, pp. 100–118). But this does not mean that nascent Christianity erased the biblical tradition in the face of the classical one, but, on the contrary, that it was innervated by the positive contribution of the latter, without in the least renouncing its biblical roots.

In fact, beyond the problems with the use of the noun *culture*, there is another problem relative to the use of the adjective *contemporary*. The meaning of this word would seem quite clear: it refers to the characteristics of the time in which the speaker lives, our own time. A frequent line casts conservatives and traditionalists as people who despise the age they live in. Perhaps some conservatives can be described in this way, but it is certainly not a constructive attitude. One who is truly educated does not despise his own age but seeks to judge it with the Catholic vision mentioned above, the sacred vision spoken of by the great Brazilian scholar Plinio Corrêa de Oliveira, which allows one not to suffer passively under the fads of the moment, but confers the power and the clarity necessary to intervene. Today, however, we are slaves to a pervasive attitude that is implicitly and covertly of Hegelian provenance (almost always through Marxist and, in Italy, Gramscian mediation). It is an evolutionist worldview, according to which whatever is more recent must necessarily be better than what proceeded it: novelty must be exalted as such, without any critical filter.

The consequences of these implicit intellectual undercurrents of our time are abundantly clear when it comes to sacred music. A presentist attitude considers only that which is immediate to be of any value; the past is to be refused and substantially ignored. In the realm of sacred music, this attitude necessarily leads to the suppression of the historical patrimony of sacred music: only music produced in the contemporary time frame is in fact capable of expressing the needs of the participants in the liturgy of the present age. This attitude is no more than the application of the dominant cancel culture of recent years, which in fact established itself in European and American culture already in the 1960s.

In the field of sacred music, a qualitative problem arises as well: Which type of "new" is to be proposed when speaking of sacred music? It is not the new of contemporary art music (and this could be debated as well), but that of commercial music, a music that is lyrically impoverished, a music whose anthropological horizon is certainly far from the vision of man evident in Catholic teaching. One must of course point out that in commercial music, in the genre of the song, not everything is of low quality: there are examples of songs that are very well composed. Unfortunately, however, the type of language adopted for the production of music for the liturgy does not correspond to the highest compositional level of commercial music (which would nevertheless be unsuitable for the liturgy) but corresponds to the second-rate commercial type, the type of musical production carried out to attract the lower instincts of people who are musically uneducated.

What good can such music do in elevating our souls to God? Above all, with what courage can this music be thought to be truly worthy of the majesty of the Creator, the Lord of Heaven and earth? This observation takes us back once more to the center of the problem, clearly described by Joseph Ratzinger in many of his works: the crisis of sacred music is rooted in the crisis of the liturgy, and the crisis of the liturgy is the manifestation of a crisis of the Catholic Faith. If we truly believed that in sacred music we are speaking with Almighty God, we would never propose the frivolity of these repertoires for use in divine worship. If we are preparing a birthday party, we look for a DJ who knows well what music is suitable for our tastes: we assess, therefore, a form of professionality. In the field of liturgical music now, we entrust the liturgy to incompetent people whose abilities are limited to scratching out a few chords on the guitar. Where do we get the courage to present ourselves before God's majesty in this way? How does this not fill us with shame?

At times we hear the response that everyone is doing the best he can, as in the Gospel passage on the poor widow who offered very little money because that was all she had, as opposed to the rich who, although offering a much larger sum, were only sacrificing a tiny portion of their vast wealth (Mark 12:41–44; Luke 21:1–4). If the poor widow had been wealthier, that little offering would not have been worthy of greater praise. Should we think that a miserly and shabby offering to God such as the cabaret production being offered for the liturgy is comparable to the widow's mite? Certainly not. The presence of serious musical professionals willing to work for the Church, the presence of adequate musical education throughout many Western nations, and economic resources that far surpasses that of past centuries, all render this prosaic sloppiness we are forced to hear in our churches simply unacceptable. This is not the widow's mite, but that of the rich man who refuses to give more. Men of the Church, you can deceive yourselves perhaps and convince yourselves of your right conscience, but you can in no way fool God.

Returning to the theme of the "desire to appear youthful" dealt with earlier, it must be pointed out here that often the musical choices described above are aimed at attracting young people. Although the ostensible aim is to attract young people, our empty pews show that this aim has not produced any fruit. There is ever greater disinterest toward religion, and contemporary music certainly has not stemmed the tide. Events such as the pilgrimage to Chartres, which in the year 2023 saw sixteen thousand people participating, display a robust presence of young people: more and more, youth are approaching forms of liturgy and traditional devotions, and esteem Gregorian chant and sacred music to a great degree. Instead of being valued as they should be, Church leaders are frightened by this trend and call these youths rigid, backward lunatics. Unfortunately, this ideological and out-of-hand rejection dominates, despite all signs pointing to a better way. Consider the success of more traditional seminaries, in sharp contrast with the emptying of seminaries in general. Obviously, no one wants to admit the colossal failure of the pastoral strategy of recent decades.

As mentioned, there exists a problematic relationship between sacred music and contemporary art music. Unfortunately, contemporary art music of the past century has dramatically detached itself from the public in the broadest sense, becoming at times a mere intellectual exercise. It has in a certain way ceased to be communicative and has become almost solipsistic for the chosen elite. Naturally, this is not true of all the art music of the past century: there are also examples of excellent composers, even brilliant ones, who have continued the mission of communicating something great and profound through their music, while utilizing a musical language that was genuinely new. What we are trying to anathematize here is not in the least the possibility of musical progress. We only seek to highlight how it has often lost its communicative ability, becoming a mere intellectual exercise for a few who consider themselves capable of understanding.

This dramatic division between the public and art music has resulted in a certain unrest in the world of sacred music as well. Although it has, as we have repeatedly emphasized, its own proper characteristics, it cannot remain indifferent to the entire stylistic situation of the world of music. The formation of church musicians also includes extensive knowledge of non-sacred repertoires, both those of classical music and those of contemporary art music. There have been musicians in the recent past who, despite the crisis of musical language, have nevertheless found their own path, both in the profane realm as well as in the sacred, maintaining normal communication with a normal public, not with a small group of acolytes.

Nevertheless, the problem of contemporary art music is profound and has to do with its inability to speak to the normal public. Little more than a century ago, the novelties of operatic music (the art music of that time) often received scores of reproductions before entering into the repertoire: there was, therefore, communication between contemporary high art and normal listeners. The direction taken by musicians of the twentieth century distanced the composer from the ordinary public, even those with a high level of sophistication, and the result was likewise an untethering of commercial music, which experienced a collapse of standards. Commercial music at the end of the nineteenth century or the beginning of the twentieth, for example, used essentially the same language as art music, although rendered more straightforward and immediate: a song was not linguistically different from an operatic aria, and there existed linguistic continuity in the musical component of consumer music, just as the texts were not linguistically different from the poetic texts of the period. The retreat of art music into a sort of inaccessible niche from normal perception isolated it and left commercial music in the hands of people quite often lacking in musical sophistication, bringing about a profound crisis.

In the field of sacred and liturgical music, the result obtained has been the dominance of the improvised musician, without any real musical education. We are not speaking of amateurs: there is a certain hesitance in using the term *amateurs* because, although *amateur* has a negative connotation, there is also a positive sense to the word, even noble I would say. Consider the great masters of the past, such as Tomaso Albinoni, who called himself "the amateur from Veneto," or Aleksandr Borodin, a chemist by profession, who dedicated his free time to music: both were musicians gifted with a solid preparation and musical sophistication. Today we are not dealing with this type of amateur but with those who, not having any adequate musical preparation, throw themselves blindly into their Christian communities to carry out a task they were not prepared to undertake.

The crisis of sacred music has its roots, therefore, in the broader crisis of art music. Unfortunately, the confusion of liturgical repertoires in the direction of mundane sloppiness is but a consequence of all this, together with the general cultural situation that we discussed above. There are also particular situations. For example, in the American scene especially, a misunderstanding regarding contemporaneity has been perpetrated. Groups that sing pop music with texts of a religious (though not always liturgical) nature are called "contemporary choirs," linking the concept of contemporaneity to a blatantly consumeristic mentality. This is a grave offense to the concept of the contemporary, whose horizon is reduced in this way to the dimension of being a product for mass consumption. This is another aspect of the failed strategy adopted in recent decades.

It has already been said that all that we have been observing here is not meant to denigrate contemporaneity in absolute terms. With its progress in the technological and scientific fields, it surely offers many new opportunities to those wishing to dedicate themselves seriously to the noble profession of the church musician. Today, it is truly possible to access a seemingly limitless quantity of documents: thanks to the Internet, a church musician today has free access to an enormous number of videos, audio files, sheet music, and books he can freely read, study, or listen to. The musician can encounter the best choirs, the most renowned organists, the greatest composers, and this offers formative possibilities previously unheard of. Naturally, the possibility of documentation does not necessarily mean an increase in sophistication and a more solid orientation. Clear guidance and direction are needed to allow one to learn from these beautiful things with constant reference to the musical tradition. What most people probably lack is discernment to aid in navigating through this immense sea of information.

Unfortunately, the Church has not been capable of taking advantage of these unprecedented possibilities, thinking that, chasing after fatuous trends, she would become more accepted by the world. But this is precisely the problem: the Church must not aspire to be accepted by the world, but her aim must be to become the "salt of the earth." In the Gospel of Matthew we read:

> You are the salt of the earth; but if salt has lost its taste, how shall its saltness be restored? It is no longer good for anything except to be thrown out and trodden under foot by men.
>
> You are the light of the world. A city on a hill cannot be hid. Nor do men light a lamp and put it under a bushel, but on a stand, and it gives light to all in the house. Let your light so shine before men, that they may see your good works and give glory to your Father who is in heaven. (5:13–16)

But can these words still be applied to the Church and her function in the world? Today the Church seems to have become for many the chaplain to the dominant powers, renouncing what is most essential to her mission. We have already spoken of the problem of Catholic education. Once, this was at the center of the pastoral practice of the Church; today, what remains of it? Very little, one seems to conclude, despite the words of great educators like the previously mentioned John Senior or, in Italy, the tradition of St. John Bosco and, more recently, Luigi Giussani. If we do not invest in an authentically Catholic culture that provides above all a solid anthropological framework, it is obvious that sacred music, like all other arts, cannot be what it is meant to be.

It is no surprise that the situation has reached its present state; the contrary would be anomalous. The ideological rejection of reality mentioned above has prevented Church leaders from comprehending the gravity of the situation; sacred music is a warning sign for a much larger shipwreck. We are truly in a situation of epochal crisis, a situation in which, seen from a merely human perspective, the end cannot be descried. Numerous lay Catholic intellectuals have emphasized this, such as Josef Seifert. We need, one would like to say, a Catholic cultural revolution, using the word *revolution* in the original sense of *revolvere*: to return. We need Church leaders who are capable of recognizing reality, who have the courage to say that we have gone in a direction that has brought nothing good, that we have distanced ourselves from what is beautiful, good, and true.

"Salt of the earth": it would surely be of great importance right now to understand how the Catholic Church, in her present state, can still be the salt of the earth, given that she has become in many aspects uninfluential. This is a legitimate question; in fact it is *the* question on which the most important reflections concerning the Catholic presence in the world are being focused. The flight of the faithful from church attendance, the downward trend of vocations, a public presence of little weight, a lack of identity, a timorous passivity toward anti-Christian ideologies: if one had just a hint of reality, one would recover the meaning of a strong Catholic identity based on the great tradition of the Church, including her liturgical and musical tradition. This is not a matter of "returning to the past" but of asking oneself: Does the Church have anything to say to the world? Or must she simply repeat the fashionable cultural mantras? In the latter case, her existence makes no sense; but we know by faith that *portae Inferi non praevalebunt*. We can deduce that the true nature of the Church can never entirely vanish.

As Ratzinger intuited in a famous conference in 1969, reiterated nearly thirty years later in his interview with Peter Seewald published under the title *The Salt of the Earth* (Ratzinger 1997a), a rediscovery of identity on the part of the Church will see a Church that is consciously a minority, the "little flock" of the Gospel. The sloppiness of the liturgy and sacred music today is the result of the Catholic world's loss of identity. Reflecting on these problems, as has already been said, does not in the least mean closing one's eyes to contemporary culture. One can take what is good and integrate it into the great tradition of the Church, as has always been done. Reference was made above to the study of Enrico Berti on Paul's discourse to the Athenians. Paul also wisely said: "Do not quench the Spirit, do not despise prophesying, but test everything; hold fast to what is good" (1 Thess. 5:19–21). The great Patristic Fathers, from Justin (second century) to Basil of Caesarea (fourth century), affirmed the necessity of dialogue with pagan culture, not to conform themselves to it but to integrate into Christianity the positive aspects of ancient Greek and Roman culture.

The Church has never been against innovation, even in sacred music. On the contrary, she was at the forefront of linguistic and musical developments for centuries, and for this reason we have our great tradition of Western music. We must not fear what is new; we must fear the void, which we are observing in many churches, where the meaning behind what they are doing has been lost. Worthy sacred music can still be written today, based on the great tradition but without rejecting the good in what modernity has to offer. Precisely in our day, such cross-pollination has become fashionable: consider what well-prepared musicians can do for music and for the liturgy by integrating several of the new possibilities in harmony and counterpoint, or even some linguistic inflexions that derive from different cultural traditions. These can be used, if one knows one's trade, without risk of profaning the sacred.

This is why church musicians should be required to know more and better their trade, and this is why practically destroying professionalism in sacred music was a tragedy that could only produce the miserable results now visible to all.

Sacred Music and Commercial Music

IN TREATING SACRED music and contemporary culture, we also touched on the theme of the relationship between sacred music and commercial music. I believe this area requires deeper reflection, because considerable confusion arises in the minds of many, and thus we should clarify our thinking.

First, some employ an argument from history: If the composers in the Renaissance used profane themes for their Masses, why is it not possible to do so today? It seems a very solid argument, but in fact it is not, because it does not stand up to the least historical scrutiny. During the Renaissance, and even previously, musical language was fundamentally homogenous: composers of profane music were the same ones who composed sacred music and the musical language was essentially the same. Furthermore, given that profane music was licentious and profoundly influenced by sacred music, one did not perceive in the musical language the enormous discrepancy one perceives today between profane music and true sacred music. One need only examine, for example, the music of great composers such as Guillaume Dufay or Josquin des Prez to notice the essential commonality of language, a unifying musical grammar, between the profane and the sacred repertoires.

There is also, more or less on the same wavelength, the argument of those who cite Psalm 150:

> *Praise the LORD!*
> *Praise God in his sanctuary;*

praise him in his mighty firmament!
Praise him for his mighty deeds;
praise him according to his exceeding greatness!

Praise him with trumpet sound;
praise him with lute and harp!
Praise him with timbrel and dance;
praise him with strings and pipe!
Praise him with sounding cymbals;
praise him with loud clashing cymbals!
Let everything that breathes praise the LORD!
Praise the LORD![51]

Here too, one affirms that the psalm refers to the use of many instruments to praise the Lord: Why not employ instruments such as the drums and the guitar for sacred music, therefore? Because at the time the Psalter was redacted, these instruments were associated with worship of God; they did not have profane resonances at that time. In 2 Chronicles 5:12–13, we find:

> And all the Levitical singers, Asaph, Heman, and Jedu'thun, their sons and kinsmen, arrayed in fine

[51] A detail regarding the translation: quite often the Greek ἐν κυμβάλοις (*en kýmbalois*, Latin *in cymbalis*) is translated "cymbals" (so runs the so-called "interconfessional translation" and that of the Italian Episcopal Conference of 1974, while the revision of 2008 corrected the error): evidently these are "cymbals," namely small percussion instruments generally made of bronze. The same observation is obviously true for other scriptural texts that use this word. The Greek word *kýmbalon* translates various names of Jewish instruments: see the accurate analysis of K. L. Schmidt in *The Great Lexicon of the New Testament* (Schmidt 1969).

> linen, with cymbals, harps, and lyres, stood east of the altar with a hundred and twenty priests who were trumpeters; and it was the duty of the trumpeters and singers to make themselves heard in unison in praise and thanksgiving to the LORD, and when the song was raised, with trumpets and cymbals and other musical instruments, in praise to the LORD, "For he is good, for his steadfast love endures for ever," the house, the house of the LORD, was filled with a cloud.

It is obviously not possible to affirm that guitars and drums present a close association with divine worship. This is so completely the case that it can be easily demonstrated by means of one of the most profane of activities: marketing. When a product is to be promoted that has some association with religion, to reinforce this association what musical genres are utilized? Certainly not songs on the guitar that we hear in many of our churches, but the organ, or a choir performing traditional sacred music. The talking heads of marketing understand this, in open contrast to not a few authoritative members of the ecclesial hierarchy.

The association of these instruments with profane music is no small problem. Profane music, especially the more commercial type, naturally aims at soliciting several particular sensations, which in some cases can be of a noble nature, but often are associated with more immediate instincts, which guarantee a more rapid grip on the consumer. The messages that are often conveyed through commercial music are those of a culture that has nothing to do with the authentic Christian message; such music proposes an anthropological model that is at odds with the Christian one. It is impossible for these melodies, even if they are covered by words that more or less correspond to liturgical needs, not to maintain a tie with the profane values that originally inspired them.

Consider the following: If we were to hear a controversial or morally unacceptable text set with a melody taken from the repertoire of Gregorian chant, we could not fail to notice a type of short circuit: the text orients the listener in one direction, while the melody points in the opposite direction, due to those associations that, as we have seen, are thoroughly exploited by marketers. The same happens when one adapts inadequate music to a liturgical text, however acceptable: an evident contrast occurs, which not only is not conducive to true and authentic liturgical prayer but rather leads to a state of great confusion. At any rate, the attentive scholar and apologist Corrado Gnerre tells us that music and other means of communication have been a key means of moral perversion:

> As concerns this latter field [that of communication], consider the musical and cinematic expressions that have become important vehicles of moral perversion. Our ways of acting and especially of thinking have undergone variations due above all to the new means of communication that have become a sounding board for the cultural revolution. (Gnerre 2013)

The same style of music that was employed for moral perversion is used in our churches today with brazen indifference. Well known in Italy, the annual Festival of Italian Song, or the Festival of San Remo (the city in which it is held), has attained enormous television success for decades, and is annually commented on for many weeks afterward throughout the national press. To the attentive observer, the songs presented at this festival (whose musical sophistication continues on a steady decline) are easily seen as vehicles for inculcating throughout society all the theories dear to the dominant culture, whether that of gender, wokeness, political correctness, cancel culture, and so forth. Sexual fluidity is not only accepted but indeed promoted at this type of spectacle.

Although it is true that there have been noble expressions in the field of commercial music, it has become an increasingly powerful means of amplification of the tendencies imposed by our anti-Christian culture, and thus an assault upon the order established by God. It makes no sense to think that a musical genre that promotes these values can also help us to pray. Furthermore, as revealed in the preceding chapter, the Church's use of this music as a promotional instrument to reach the youth has resulted in a complete failure.

It seems that not a few currents active in the Catholic Church function as regurgitators of the trends of the dominant culture. We are not advocating ignoring these cultural expressions: they must certainly be studied even for the sake of defending ourselves from possible dangers. Unfortunately, however, we are witnessing in the actions of some prelates a phenomenon of acquiescence toward this culture, almost a kind of admiration. One significant example is found in pop theology. A simple documentation online shows that pop theology is defined as the encounter between religion and pop culture. How can pop culture be defined? For the most part, it is a form of culture imposed by multinational corporations whose only aim is to increase profits using all the means at their disposal, including those of subliminal messaging through marketing.

In Italy, an eminent representative of this theological current is Msgr. Antonio Staglianò, who has dedicated various books to this theme. In *Pop Theology for Young People*, Msgr. Staglianò presents a very clear synthesis of the tendency of this type of thought. In the preface to the book, we read:

> Man is slowly being reduced to consumption, commodity, number, mass. Yet human beings are extraordinary, imaginative, creative, and highly successful in the field of technology. However, in the realm of love, they appear lacking, disappointed, and frustrated. Made for love, it is precisely love that fails. Why? The answer can be found in Renato Zero's latest song *Gesù*: "Jesus, we no longer resemble you." When humanity distances itself from the humanity of Jesus, "the earth is on its knees, alone more alone than ever." In the current conditions of fear in today's world, struck by the barbarism of international terrorism disguised as fundamentalist religion, it is necessary to present to young people, with intelligence and humility, the human model of Jesus, his humanity rich in love and peace, tolerance and dedication, trust and positivity, beautiful, and full of the good energies of every human being. Pop theology, as "popular theology," takes on the task of critically thinking about "traditional Catholicism," rejuvenating Christian preaching, so that faith does not risk becoming just a religious mask without reference to the God of Jesus and His humanity. It is *pop* theology, intellectual charity, knowing that today's youth express themselves with their own particular language, that of music.

This is certainly an approach founded on a praiseworthy intention, that of reaching the generation born at the end of the twentieth century or the beginning of the twenty-first. But one must note the naïveté behind it, based on the implicit conviction that what it calls the "language of young people" can be adopted in an indifferent manner, as if language were not as such an intrinsic manifestation of a way of viewing the world. And we must not assume that this is something that can be ignored with superficial indifference, because Msgr. Staglianò enjoys the highest esteem; in fact, in 2022, Pope Francis nominated him president of the Pontifical Academy of Theology, a very high responsibility. Staglianò returned to these themes, in particular to the use of consumer music, in his 2020 work *On the Notes of God* (Staglianò 2020).

The example we just read offers us an instrument for understanding how much of contemporary theological thought is characterized by a fundamental ambiguity that is not difficult to identify. On one side, it denounces the fact that man is reduced to merchandise, consumption, a number, and so on. On the other, it presumes to use linguistic and musical instruments that foster this process and are a constituent part of it, like commercial music, a vehicle of anti-Christian values and ideas. The misunderstanding was fomented by equating pop theology and popular theology. It is not clear what is meant by popular theology, given that people who are true and authentic are not interested in theological research: they live the faith, they do not theorize it; they live the faith in ways at times beautiful and authentic, at times contaminated by ideas that are entirely distorted. Think of the example of Japanese Christians who during the persecution of Catholicism remained for centuries without priests: many of them provided extraordinary examples of Christian heroism and should be admired unreservedly. But we also know that others, though remaining attached to the religion, began introducing elements that were entirely extraneous to it. This case shows how problematic it can be to speak of popular theology. If this theology is the fruit of consumeristic cultural artifacts, how can we maintain our criticism of the reduction of man to a mere consumer?

Returning to the discussion of music, when one speaks of the people's music, one means a type of music that flowed directly and spontaneously from the people, who shared a common identity and tradition, above all in the context of peasant civilizations, which have produced a bounty of religious songs, often of great beauty. The type of music of interest to this sort of theological approach certainly does not present these characteristics, but is rather the work of professionals and experts skilled in marketing, who are paid to produce music and sell as much as possible using every means at their disposal (authentic popular music was certainly extraneous to the logic of the market, belonging as it did to a different level of social organization).

It is worth noting once again some points discussed in previous chapters, but which should be clearer after what we have examined here:

1. The concentration of theological and pastoral concerns against alleged "conventional Catholicism," understood as traditional Catholicism, does not seem to have obtained the desired results: practicing Catholics are fewer than ever, vocations are scarce, and the authority of the Church as a bearer of her particular vision has been greatly weakened.

2. The attempt to appear youthful has not obtained the least effect. What most impresses those working in education, from schools to universities, is not the perception of hostility toward the Church as much as her total superfluousness. The search for a "youthful language," although stemming from good intentions, has revealed itself to be an essentially naïve attitude: this presumed language is in fact the result of very effective cultural-commercial constructs. Like any language, it cannot be a neutral instrument, but necessarily carries with it a certain vision of the world.

3. From a musical point of view, we have no intention of criticizing in a superficial manner the genre of the pop song. We are well aware that there are in this genre examples of notable artistic craftsmanship. But in this case as well, these products obey a logic that is not and cannot be considered compatible with authentic sacred music. This is not only a problem of quality but also a problem of opportunity.

As said previously, the well-prepared composer of sacred music will certainly know how to integrate the stimuli that come even from the secular sphere into sacred liturgical music, without however allowing these stimuli to desacralize the music. To do this, a profound understanding of sacred music is needed: knowledge of its techniques, history, and tradition obtained over years and years of study. Unfortunately, the possibility of having professional musicians who dedicate their lives to sacred music has vanished in many places, and thus its growth has been inhibited. This has been catastrophic for music and for the liturgy.

Must one think that the people of our age are incapable of appreciating beauty and traditional solemnity, preferring commercial music? Even if this were true (and it is not), it would nonetheless be the Church's duty to educate people to the true sense of the liturgy and the role of sacred music in it. We have already said how the collapse of the Church's pedagogical mechanism has led to such grave consequences. It is a matter of the "path of beauty" that the Anglican thinker Roger Scruton testified to so many times. But at the moment, even within the Catholic world, this is a perspective whose temporal horizon is still out of sight, for the Church should educate first her own clergy, who for the most part have become inured to a liturgy and to music deformed by the sloppiness of a worldly and profaning mentality.

In the depths of the truly popular sensibility there lies hidden an aspiration to something that in some way surpasses the triviality and usury of consumeristic daily life. In the previous chapter, we cited the enormous success that the pilgrimage to Chartres has had in terms of youth participation: its organizers in 2023 were forced to close registration early, due to an overwhelming response. The pilgrimage concluded with a Pontifical Mass in Latin, celebrated by the bishop of Chartres. The ceremony was characterized not only by the splendor of the rite but also by high-quality music with wide popular participation. Outside of the Catholic world as well, one perceives this need for a space that lifts man up from the frivolity of daily life, cadenced by the cycle of work, consumption, and yet more work.

The enormous interest aroused by the coronation ceremony of King Charles III in London on May 6, 2023, comes to mind. From the reactions on social media, one clearly senses the admiration of millions of people (among them many Catholics) for the solemnity and the beauty of the ceremony and the sacred music, which was performed in exemplary fashion. Many aspects of this ceremony were criticized by Anglicans as well as Catholics: it was obviously the rite of a non-Catholic Christian confession, during which the new king reiterated his commitment to the entire Protestant world. But the visual beauty, beyond the auditory beauty of the whole rite, did not fail to strike the souls of many who no longer find such things in our own liturgies.

A marginal reflection on this media event reveals a hidden wealth in the Catholic tradition. Certainly, as regards the British monarchy, the ascension to certain roles is conditioned by belonging to the royal family. But for the Catholic Church this is not the case. An example of a Catholic rite celebrated with great solemnity and sacred music was that of the 1958 coronation of Pope John XXIII. This ceremony was chosen because it can still be admired on YouTube: obviously the quality of the video and audio is that of sixty years ago, but one comprehends the solemnity and the beauty realized there. We find it evocative to imagine that ceremony filmed with the video and audio technologies available today: it would truly be comparable to that of the coronation of the British royals. But in the pope's case, John XXIII did not belong to a royal family: he was the son of humble farmers. This is not an isolated case, either: those who remember the Pontifical Mass of Cardinal Giuseppe Siri remember well the solemnity of the rite, the beauty of the music entrusted to maestros of the highest quality, the simple majesty of those liturgies: a prince of the Church rose to the altar, the son of two humble caretakers, not from a royal family.

John Henry Newman, in his novel *Loss and Gain*, tells in an indirect way of his own conversion, narrating the stupor admired by the young Anglican protagonist, who for the first time attended a Catholic liturgy and saw that everyone played their part—from the singing of the celebrant, to the choir, to the faithful singing, to the organist—in simple unaffectedness, like in some grand instrumental band. And he remarked, "*This* is a popular religion." One encounters the true people not by lowering the music and the liturgy to quotidian drivel but by raising the soul, darkly thirsting for beauty and truth, beyond the grayness of the world and toward the light.

Confronting Failure

FROM WHAT EMERGES in the preceding chapters, the conclusion seems inevitable that the situation of sacred music in the Catholic Church is desperate. One must not think that certain havens do not exist, but unfortunately, they are very few, and at times they find themselves at odds with members of the clergy. It is of course quite saddening to realize that part of the clergy, which should be on the forefront of promoting the development of true sacred music and the dignity of the liturgy, are accomplices to their destruction. Besides those few havens of beauty, the situation is appalling. We must not be afraid to declare that these recent years of reforms (often savage) have ended in a comprehensive failure, and this acknowledgement is the necessary condition for glimpsing the hope of a recovery and a new beginning. How much can one hope that the Catholic hierarchy admits that the reforms in liturgy and music, whatever good intentions might have motivated them, have been a complete disaster? Unfortunately, this hope is nearly nonexistent. On the contrary, we observe how they struggle with ever greater obstinacy to impose the narrative of post-conciliar success, and fight in every way the various expressions of our great tradition in the liturgical and musical fields.

Must we then fall into desperation and abandon the barque of Peter? This is a temptation for many, a temptation one can even understand, but that cannot be justified in the final analysis. If we believe that the Catholic Church possesses the fullness of truth, which comes from Christ, belonging to her is not negotiable. Disappointment with the disintegration of Catholic identity can push one to seek refuge in other faiths, but we are speaking here of our own eternal life or damnation. This is not like changing allegiance from one football team to another. No team possesses the truth; the true Church of Christ *does* possess the Truth. This is not an attempt to deny the disorientation that many feel in this present situation of loss of identity and accommodation to the mainstream of the dominant culture: this disorientation is quite understandable. But if we abandon the Catholic Church, we will never find the full truth in any other confession.

Once more, we turn to the witness of one of the greats of the modern Church, John Henry Newman. As a young scholar and newly ordained Anglican priest, Newman was inclined to hold that Roman Catholicism, Orthodoxy, and Anglicanism represented different expressions of the patrimony of an essentially unitary faith. But his study of fourth-century Arianism convinced him that only Roman Catholicism was the integral custodian of the patrimony of the Faith of the Fathers, and for this reason he became a Catholic. The choice, therefore, was not between the Catholic Church and other confessions but between belief and unbelief. If you believe, then you must go where the truth revealed in Christ dwells, and that means in the Church He founded. If you do not believe, then it is better to embrace atheism than a lie. Unfortunately, as stated above, this is a real source of suffering for many, a weight with which they must live, trying to find the strength to bear what by human resources seems unbearable.

There are too many people, including clerics, who have been completely deformed and miseducated over recent decades. How guilty can they really be? Even many of us who have grown up in the post-conciliar period have received a type of deformation that considers the Mass to be a sort of party. Then we had the good fortune (or misfortune, if we see it from another perspective) of understanding that we had been misled, that most of what we observe in our churches is not in line with the true Catholic tradition. This of course creates a profound sense of consternation and makes many of the faithful feel uprooted: we seem to be unwanted guests in the very Church that welcomed us in Baptism. And yet this must not diminish our courage in the fight for what we hold to be good and holy, in the fight for the prerogatives of God that have been trampled upon in recent decades: God's right to be worthily worshipped and praised with music that is not the mere regurgitation of the worship of Mammon. Catholic musicians will be recognized in their goodwill in collaborating with the clergy, but also in being firm in their convictions when these are based on the true Tradition of the Church. Members of the clergy need to comprehend that they are not the masters of the liturgy but rather, we might say, its administrators. The liturgy has been entrusted to them; they did not invent it. If the liturgy does not come from God, it is only a human invention, and in that case the creativity of chance and improvisation can function well; not so if the liturgy is a patrimony that is bequeathed to us via Sacred Tradition from God Himself.

The bishop, as evidenced in the etymology of his title, is "one who oversees and safeguards."[52] Neither is the bishop the master of the liturgy: the bishops, and with them the pope, are accountable to a higher and infinitely more powerful authority. But if the phrase *prima sedes a nemine iudicatur* is true, it is likewise true that the task of feeding the flock is preeminently the role entrusted to the Holy Father, and to the bishops in communion with the Apostolic See. They cannot legislate in a manner that, distancing themselves from the Tradition and from Scripture, would harm

[52] "Supervisor or custodian is the best translation of the term ἐπίσκοπος": Beyer 1967, col. 756.

the people of God in their faith, or mislead them or deceive them. If in good conscience even the simplest layperson considers magisterial acts to be erroneous, he has the possibility, and in some ways the duty, to articulate his considered evaluation. The *Catechism of the Catholic Church* mentions *correctio fraterna* (nos. 1435 and 1829) and treats at length the conscience and its freedom (nos. 1776–1802). In a short discourse in 2005, commenting on the dictate of St. Paul to "encourage one another" (*exortamini invicem*), Benedict XVI defined fraternal correction as an "act of mercy": none of us is capable of "seeing himself or his shortcomings clearly"; we need help to "see better."[53]

The *Code of Canon Law* also assures the faithful of the possibility, and in some ways the duty, to express to their pastors their observations on the direction undertaken by the Church:

> According to the knowledge, competence, and prestige which they possess, they have the right and even at times the duty to manifest to the sacred pastors their opinion on matters which pertain to the good of the Church and to make their opinion known to the rest of the Christian faithful, without prejudice to the integrity of faith and morals, with reverence toward their pastors, and attentive to common advantage and the dignity of persons. (Canon 212, para. 3)

We see clearly in this canon how the right to express one's opinion has as its presupposition the preservation of the integrity of the Faith. As we have seen in preceding chapters, we can conclude that

[53] Discourse on October 3, 2005, available at https://www.vatican.va/content/benedict-xvi/en/speeches/2005/october/documents/hf_ben_xvi_spe_20051003_synod-bishops.html.

the current condition of sacred music represents a threat to the integrity of the Faith, due to the elimination of the sense of the sacred and the adoration that should constitute the continual nourishment that our spiritual life draws from sacred art. Desacralized liturgy and music, in fact, no longer carries out the function of elevating the faithful to the contemplation of spiritual things; above all, these things are gravely offensive to God's majesty.

Therefore, we need laypeople who are well formed, educated, and above all courageous. Unfortunately, a form of clericalism is quite common, and it is, as Pope Francis has observed on various occasions, characteristic of not a few priests. But there is also a clericalism of Catholic laity, an acquiescence to choices that they know to be erroneous, out of fear of losing prestigious opportunities or careers. In this sense, even some church musicians are not without fault when they renounce serving God in order to serve this or that priest, this or that bishop, and remain silent in the face of obvious profanations of the liturgy, because they are more attached to their own career than to their artistic and personal integrity.

Certainly, the new possibilities offered by technology, with new and immediate means of communication, constitute a tremendous opportunity to those who struggle to make their voice heard and to spread their views in an effective manner. On the other hand, they present a serious risk: as Umberto Eco observed at the start of the social media explosion, the web lowers to the same level the chatter at the coffee shop and the intervention of a Nobel Prize winner, promoting the reign of imbecility. Consider the innumerable educational possibilities available through YouTube, Facebook, Twitter, and so forth. One must be able to discern what is useful and what is merely background noise and idle talk.

The attentive and continual study of the great musical tradition of the Catholic Church, beginning with Gregorian chant, constitutes an essential activity for a church musician. Unfortunately, space is given today to people who have not received adequate formation and who therefore believe that sacred music is that which they have been subjected to since their youth. Nearly everyone born after the 1960s has been exposed to that type of "sacred" music that we have discussed and criticized thus far; the same can be said of many priests and even bishops of the same generations. To return to good sense, we must hope for a return to the healthy tradition, to listening to the great inheritance that our fathers have bequeathed us: not out of nostalgia for a past that by now almost no one can remember but in order to build on solid foundations a future with meaning. We need the courage of the tradition; we need to know it and listen to it to draw from it the inspiration necessary to build something new. This attitude is countercultural today, and even dangerous in a certain sense: whoever steps out of the mainstream knows he is moving toward being marginalized. Better at any rate to run this risk and remain in the truth, rather than to be successful in a lie.

But this certainly does not deny that the problems for a church musician wanting to remain faithful to the essentials of his mission are truly enormous. We have already mentioned what is most likely the greatest problem of all: relationships with most of the clergy. This is nothing new: an article from 1997 described this situation already in the form of a narrative "sketch,"[54] and after twenty-five years the change is certainly toward a further stabilization of this reality, after the passage of almost an entire generation. Unfortunately, the clergy is increasingly in need of

[54] See Milanese 1997. This short article, originally published in the journal of choral music *La Cartellina*, had unexpected success and was reproduced on many websites, without the author's permission for its reproduction.

education in the field of liturgy, and even more so in that of music. In many seminaries, not even a word of Latin is taught, rendering the relationship with sacred music quite complicated. This miseducation is clearly contrary to all that the texts of Vatican II called for, and it is quite sad that these choices are actually presented as applications of Vatican II. The result is that the clergy is almost inevitably led to make decisions in the matter that are entirely inadequate, placing serious obstacles before those who seek to carry out the task assigned to them with dignity and respect for the liturgy. This is one of the greatest tragedies for the Catholic Church. A liturgy disfigured by that disordered "creativity" and by the need to be at the center of attention, as Ratzinger pointed out already in the 1980s, does not constitute an environment that can accommodate sacred music, and in the final analysis, it does not help in building the life of the Faith.

One must ask why the Church, in light of a liturgical reform like the one following Vatican II, did not carry out what was required by promoting adequate liturgical and musical formation, continuing to train her priests in the tradition while at the same time opening herself up to new needs. In this way she could have guaranteed the organic development of the liturgy and sacred music that is at the center of *Sacrosanctum Concilium* and all the Magisterium's teaching, ensuring the preservation of the necessary dignity and solemnity of the celebration, and of its "integral part," as Vatican II felicitously calls sacred music. Of course, we must understand how priests today are also the sons of modern society: they too, then, have been formed in this culture, with all of its great limitations. This is no doubt true, but in reality, it would be an even greater reason for requiring a more rigorous formation that protects from the many dangers that arise from the profane environment and can provide the clergy with the capacity to enter into dialogue with the surrounding world without being overwhelmed.

The scarcity of vocations is such a serious problem that there is a risk of accepting candidates without sufficient discernment. It is worthwhile to observe that institutes of formation with a traditional orientation, whether in a regular canonical situation such as the Priestly Fraternity of St. Peter, or in an irregular canonical situation such as the Society of St. Pius X, are receiving abundant vocations and ordain scores of new priests every year who follow a rigorous itinerary of studies. Can the path toward a recovery of sacred music arise from these institutes? As concerns Gregorian chant, the foundation of sacred music, it is difficult to see this happening, at least at the present moment.

Unfortunately, in many of these institutes, the study of Gregorian chant is based on reference to manuals they mistakenly consider "traditional," while in reality they only reflect the popular practice that dominated for a brief period from around 1910 to 1970. During that period, a particular rhythmic theory (inappropriately said to be of Solesmes) was diffused through volumes in general use in those decades by the clergy, such as the famous *Liber Usualis*. This is not, therefore, a traditional way of singing, but only the method that spread in the first half of the twentieth century, with the aim of allowing all priests to sing a repertoire, Gregorian chant, which in fact requires serious preparation. Dom Jean Claire, director of the abbey choir of Solesmes for many years, clarified that what came to be called the "method of Solesmes" was never followed there (Claire 1990).[55]

[55] An immense bibliography of treatises, manuals, and introductions flourished around these theories, all in some way dependent on the great work of Dom André Mocquereau, *Le nombre musical grégorien* (Mocquereau 1908). The Ward Foundation is still active today in spreading

Poor liturgical and musical preparation leads many priests to hardening their positions precisely because they have not had any occasion for contact with the great musical tradition of the Church. As explained above, the appeal at Vatican II to justify the banalization of sacred music is unfounded: Vatican II offered precise and clear words on the role of sacred music, Latin, and the education of the clergy. We cannot forget the words of Benedict XVI in his famous discourse on December 22, 2005, for his Christmas greeting to the Roman Curia:

> The question arises: Why has the implementation of the Council, in large parts of the Church, thus far been so difficult?
>
> Well, it all depends on the correct interpretation of the Council or—as we would say today—on its proper hermeneutics, the correct key to its interpretation and application. The problems in its implementation arose from the fact that two contrary hermeneutics came face to face and quarreled with each other. One caused confusion, the other, silently but more and more visibly, bore and is bearing fruit.
>
> On the one hand, there is an interpretation that I would call "a hermeneutic of discontinuity and rupture"; it has frequently availed itself of the sympathies of the mass media, and also one trend of modern theology. On the other, there is the "hermeneutic of reform," of renewal in the continuity of

---

the method in the United States: see https://music.catholic.edu/faculty-and-research/areas-of-research/ward-method-studies/ward-method/index.html.

the one subject-Church which the Lord has given to us. She is a subject which increases in time and develops, yet always remaining the same, the one subject of the journeying People of God.

The hermeneutic of discontinuity risks ending in a split between the pre-conciliar Church and the post-conciliar Church. It asserts that the texts of the Council as such do not yet express the true spirit of the Council. It claims that they are the result of compromises in which, to reach unanimity, it was found necessary to keep and reconfirm many old things that are now pointless. However, the true spirit of the Council is not to be found in these compromises but instead in the impulses toward the new that are contained in the texts.

These innovations alone were supposed to represent the true spirit of the Council, and starting from and in conformity with them, it would be possible to move ahead. Precisely because the texts would only imperfectly reflect the true spirit of the Council and its newness, it would be necessary to go courageously beyond the texts and make room for the newness in which the Council's deepest intention would be expressed, even if it were still vague.

In a word: it would be necessary not to follow the texts of the Council but its spirit. In this way, obviously, a vast margin was left open for the question on how this spirit should subsequently be defined and room was consequently made for every whim.

The nature of a Council as such is therefore basically misunderstood. In this way, it is considered

> as a sort of constituent that eliminates an old constitution and creates a new one. However, the Constituent Assembly needs a mandator and then confirmation by the mandator, in other words, the people the constitution must serve. The Fathers had no such mandate and no one had ever given them one; nor could anyone have given them one because the essential constitution of the Church comes from the Lord and was given to us so that we might attain eternal life and, starting from this perspective, be able to illuminate life in time and time itself.[56]

This text has not been without criticism and contestations. But I believe that for our purposes it is interesting to highlight the framework that the pope (who participated at the Second Vatican Council as a peritus) draws with respect to those who presume that Vatican II was a new beginning that erased everything that preceded it. Naturally, this attitude had devastating consequences on the liturgy and sacred music, consequences that we are still seeing today.

It is not easy to imagine a positive future for sacred music in the liturgical and musical climate in which we are living. In a famous discourse half a century ago, referring to the "smoke of Satan entering the temple," Paul VI observed:

> One believed that after the Council a day of sunlight for the history of the Church would arrive. Instead, a

[56] Benedict XVI, Address of His Holiness Benedict XVI to the Roman Curia Offering Them His Christmas Greetings, December 2005, https://www.vatican.va/content/benedict-xvi/en/speeches/2005/december/documents/hf_ben_xvi_spe_20051222_roman-curia.html.

> day of clouds, of storms, of darkness, of searching, and of uncertainty has come. We preach ecumenism and we are increasingly alienated from others. Rather than fill abysses, we are trying to dig them.[57]

Fifty years later, we are living through a time in which the Church is tossed about by thousands of problems. The only hope is that God might intervene to straighten the rudder and bring the barque of Peter, in all the splendor of her liturgy and her music, back to a safe course. To conclude our discussion of this topic, we point to a task that falls to all of us, laypeople and members of the clergy alike, who have competence in this field and who want to place ourselves trustingly and generously at the service of the Church. We can once more cite the words of Pope Paul VI:

> Let us say that the Church needs to be constructed; it needs to be restored, to be built, to be enlarged. The complex plan of her construction has not yet been executed.[58]

Restore, build, enlarge: this can be the motto of the musician who wants to serve the Church today through sacred music. And may the great suffering that the musician must undergo to remain faithful to the great musical tradition of the Church be repaid one day.

[57] The Italian original is available at https://www.vatican.va/content/paul-vi/it/homilies/1972/documents/hf_p-vi_hom_19720629.html.

[58] The Italian original is available at https://www.vatican.va/content/paul-vi/it/audiences/1966/documents/hf_p-vi_aud_19661207.html.

Bibliography

Amerio, Romano (1996). *Iota Unum: A Study of the Changes in the Catholic Church in the Twentieth Century*. Kansas City: Angelus.

Antonelli, Cristiana (1988). "Maqam Compositions in Latin Liturgical Repertoires." In *Music and Liturgy in Mediterranean Culture: Acts from the International Convention of Studies (Venice, 2–5 October 1985)*. Ed. Piero G. Arcangeli. *Notebooks of the Italian Journal of Musicology* (Italian Society of Musicology) 20. Florence: Olschki, pp. 177–184.

Bassi, A. (1994). "Gaspare Spontini and the Reform of Church Music." In *Rivista internationale di musica sacra* 15, pp. 271–279.

Bergeron, Katherine (1998). *Decadent Enchantments: The Revival of Gregorian Chant at Solesmes*. Berkeley: University of California Press.

Berry, Mary (2001). "John XXII [Duèse, Jacques]." In *Grove Music Online*. https://www.oxfordmusiconline.com/grovemusic/view/10.1093/gmo/9781561592630.001.0001/omo-9781561592630-e-0000014386. Oxford University Press.

Berti, Enrico (2020). *Saggi di storia della filosofia* [*Essays on the History of Philosophy*]. Rome: Edizioni Studium.

Bianchi, Lorenzo (2002). *Liturgia. Memoria o istruzioni per l'uso? Studi sulla trasformazione della lingua dei testi liturgici nell'attuazione della riforma* [*Liturgy: Memory or Instruction Manual? Studies on the Transformation of the Language of the Liturgical Texts in Carrying Out the Reform*]. Casale Monferrato: Edizioni Piemme.

Botte, Bernard (1935). *Le canon de la messe romaine* [*The Canon of the Roman Mass*]. Louvain: Abbaye du Mont César.

Botte, Bernard, and Christine Mohrmann (1953). *L'Ordinaire de la messe* [*The Ordinary of the Mass*]. Paris: Éditions de Cerf.

Bugnini, Annibale (1949). "Per una riforma liturgica generale" [*For a General Liturgical Reform*]. In *Ephemerides Liturgicae* 63, pp. 165–184.

——— (1983). *La Riforma liturgica* [*The Liturgical Reform*] *(1948–1975)*. Rome: LV. Edizioni liturgiche.

Calliari, Giuseppe (2022). *Laurence Feininger. Un cammino di vita alla ricerca del sublime tra arte, musica e fede*. [*Laurence Feininger: A Life's Path in Search of the Sublime in Art, Music, and Faith*] Trent: TeSto.

Cardine, Dom Eugène (1970). *Sémiologie grégorienne*. Solesmes: Abbaye Saint-Pierre de Solesmes.

——— (1979). *Semiologia gregoriana* [*Gregorian Semiology*]. Ed. G. Joppich and R. Fischer. Second ed. Rome: Pontifical Institute of Sacred Music

Casadei Turroni Monti, Mauro (2011). *Lettere dal fronte ceciliano: Le visioni di don Guerrino Amelli nei carteggi conservati a S. Maria del Monte di Cesena* [*Letters from the Cecilian Front: The Visions of Don Guerrino Amelli in the Records Conserved in Santa Maria del Monte in Cesena*]. Florence: L. S. Olschki.

Casadei Turroni Monti, Mauro, and Cesarino Ruini, curators (2004). *Aspetti del cecilianesimo nella cultura musicale italiana dell'Ottocento* [*Aspects of the Cecilian Movement in Italian Musical Culture of the Eighteenth Century*]. *Monumenta studia instrumenta liturgica* 36. Vatican City: Libreria Editrice Vaticana.

Cattin, Giulio (1984). *Music of the Middle Ages 1*. Translated by Steven Botterill. Cambridge: Cambridge University Press.

——— (1991). *La monodia nel medioevo* [*Monody in the Middle Ages*]. Turin: EDT.

Claire, Jean (1990). "Fifty Years of Gregorian Studies at Solesmes." In *Boll. Associaz. Internaz. Studi Canto Gregoriano* 15, pp. 9–27.

Clerck, Paul De (1994). "'Lex Orandi, Lex Credendi': The Original Sense and Historical Avatars of an Equivocal Adage." In *Studia Liturgica* 24.2, pp. 178–200.

Combe, Pierre (2003). *The Restoration of Gregorian Chant: Solesmes and the Vatican Edition*. English trans. by Theodore N. Marier and William Skinner. Washington, D.C.: Catholic University of America Press.

Confucius (2014). *The Analects*. Trans. Simon Leys. New York: W. W. Norton and Co.

Crossley-Holland, Peter (1976). "The Ritual Music of Tibet." In *The Tibet Journal* 1.3/4, pp. 45–54.

Davies, Michael (1976). *Cranmer's Godly Order: The Destruction of Catholicism through Liturgical Change*. Dickinson, Texas: Angelus Press.

——— (2003). *Liturgical Time Bombs in Vatican II*. Rockford, IL: TAN Books.

della Croce, Theodossios Maria (2001). *Scoprire l'altro universo: La via sacra della redenzione* [*Discovering the Other Universe: The Sacred Road to Redemption*]. Third ed. Rome: Città Nuova.

de Mattei, Roberto (2019). *Il Concilio Vaticano II: Una storia mai scritta* [*Vatican II: A History That Was Never Written*]. Second ed. Turin: Lindau.

——— (2009). *La liturgia della Chiesa nell'epoca della secolarizzazione*. [*The Liturgy of the Church in the Age of Secularization*]. Chieti: Solfanelli.

Denecker, Tim (2018). "Among Latinists: Alfred Ernout and Einar Löfstedt's Responses to the 'Nijmegen School' and Its Christian Sondersprache Hypothesis." In *Historiographia Linguistica* 45, pp. 325–362.

Dessì, Paola, and Antonio Lovato, curators. (2017). *Giovanni Tebaldini (1864–1952) e la restituzione della musica antica* [*Giovanni*

Tebaldini (1864–1952) and the Restitution of Ancient Music]. *Centro Studi Antoniani* 61. Padua: Centro Studi Antoniani.

Drumbl, Johann (1981). *Quem quaeritis: teatro sacro dell'alto Medioevo* [*Quem Quaeritis: The Sacred Theater of the High Middle Ages*]. Rome: Bulzoni.

——— (2003). "Studien zum *Codex Buranus*." In *Aevum* 77, pp. 323–356.

English–Latin Roman Missal (1966). New York: Betzinger Brothers.

Fellerer, K. Gustav (1967). "Gregorian Chant, the Flemmish, and the Reform in the Music of Palestrina." In *Nuova Riv. Music. Ital.* 1, pp. 449–464.

Fellerer, K. G., and Moses Hadas (1953). "Church Music and the Council of Trent." In *The Musical Quarterly* 39, pp. 576–594.

Foley, Edward (1984). *Music in Ritual: A Pre-Theological Investigation*. Washington, D.C.: Pastoral Press.

——— (2009). *Foundations of Christian Music: The Music of Pre-Constantinian Christianity*. Piscataway, NJ: Gorgias Press.

Fubini, Enrico (1994). *La musica nella tradizione ebraica* [*Music in Jewish Tradition*]. Turin: Einaudi.

——— (2012). *Musica e canto nella mistica ebraica* [*Music and Song in Jewish Mysticism*]. Florence: Giuntina.

Gallo, F. Alberto (1991). *La polifonia nel Medioevo* [*Polyphony in the Middle Ages*]. Second revised edition. Turin: EDT.

Gnerre, Corrado (2013). *La rivoluzione nell'uomo: una lettura anche teologica del '68* [*The Revolution in Man: A Theological Reading of 1968*]. Introduction by Roberto de Mattei. Verona: Fede e Cultura.

Gozzi, Marco (2010). "On the Need for a New Edition of the *Cortona Laudario*." In *Philomusica Online* 9.2, pp. 114–174.

Hwang, Alexander Y. (2010). "Prosper, Cassian, and Vincent: The Rule of Faith in the Augustinian Controversy." In *Tradition and the Rule of Faith in the Early Church: Essays in Honor of Joseph T. Lienhard, S.J.* Edited by Ronnie J. Rombs and Alexander Y. Hwang. Washington, D.C.: Catholic University of America Press, pp. 68–88.

Idelsohn, Abraham Zebi (2011). *Jewish Music in Its Historical Development.* New York: Dover.

Jeffery, Peter (1992). *Re-envisioning Past Musical Cultures: Ethnomusicology in the Study of Gregorian Chant.* Chicago: University of Chicago Press.

Kittel, Gerhard, and Gerhard Freidrich, curators (1967). *Grande lessico del Nuovo Testamento* [*The Great Lexicon of the New Testament*]. Brescia: Paideia.

Kurkdjian, Gérard (2016). *Le grand livre des musiques sacrées du monde* [*The Great Book of World Sacred Music*]. Paris: Albin Michel.

Kvaalvaag, Robert W. (2019). *God of Time and Space: New Perspectives on Bob Dylan and Religion.* Cappelen Damm Akademisk/NOASP (Nordic Open Access Scholarly Publishing).

Lang, Uwe Michael (2003). *Conversi ad Dominum. Zu Geschichte und Theologie der christlichen Gebetsrichtung* [*Conversi ad Dominum: On the History and Theology of Christian Prayer Direction*]. Introduction by Joseph Cardinal Ratzinger. Freiburg: Johannes Verlag Einsiedeln.

——— (2012). *The Voice of the Church at Prayer: Reflections on Liturgy and Language.* San Francisco: Ignatius Press.

——— (2022). *The Roman Mass: From Early Christian Origins to Tridentine Reform.* Cambridge: Cambridge University Press.

Livi, Antonio, and Aurelio Porfiri (2018). *Dogma, teologia e pastorale: Un teologo parla* [*Dogma, Theology, and Pastoral Care: A Theologian Speaks*] Hong Kong: Chorabooks.

Maltby, Robert (1991). *A Lexicon of Ancient Latin Etymologies*. Leeds: Fr. Cairns.

Milanese, Guido (1997). "Peccato, Maestro!... Ma come, Maestro! Latino, gregoriano, musica sacra oggi" [Too Bad, Professor!... How Come, Professor! Latin, Gregorian, Sacred Music Today]. In *La Cartellina*, pp. 3–12.

——— (2005). "Da Pustet al tradizionalismo del 2000" [*From Pustet to the Traditionalism of 2000*]. In *Musica e storia* 13, pp. 515–529.

——— (2014a). "Newman and Gregorian Chant." In *Antiphon* 20.2 (2016), pp. 123–150.

——— (2014b). "Sondaggi su grafie gregoriane e suono del latino" [*Surveys on Gregorian Handwriting and the Sound of Latin*]. In *Latinitas: Commentarii Linguae Latinae Excolendae Provehendae* 2, pp. 51–68.

——— (2015). "La pronuncia del latino e il canto gregoriano: note d'insieme" [*Latin Pronunciation and Gregorian Chant: Overview Notes*]. In *Studi Gregoriani* 31, pp. 63–82.

Mocquereau, Dom André (1908). *Le nombre musical grégorien, ou rhythmique gregorienne, théorie, et pratique* [*The Gregorian Musical Number, or Gregorian Rhythm, Theory, and Practice*]. Rome: Societè Saint Jean l'Evangeliste, Desclee.

Mohrmann, Christine (1957). *Liturgical Latin: Its Origins and Character*. Three lectures (delivered on May 8, 9, and 10, 1957, at the Catholic University of America). Washington, D.C.: Catholic University of America Press.

——— (1965). *Études sur le latin des chrétiens* [*Studies on Christian Latin*]. Vol. 3: *Latin chrétien et liturgique*. Rome: Edizioni di storia e letteratura.

Newman, John Henry (2012). *Loss and Gain*. San Francisco: Ignatius Press.

O'Callaghan, Donal (1983). "A Brudevaelte Lur Re-Examined: The Evidence for Ritual Music in the Scandinavian Late Bronze Age." In *The Galpin Society Journal* 36, pp. 104–108.

Otto, Rudolf (1917). *Das Heilige: Über das Irrationale in der Idee des Göttlichen und sein Verhältnis zum Rationalen* [*The Sacred: On the Irrational in the Idea of the Divine and Its Relationship to the Rational*]. Breslau: Trewendt & Granier.

Penyeh, Tsao, and Shi Xinming (1992). "Current Research of Daoist Ritual Music in Mainland China and Hong Kong." In *Annual for Traditional Music* 24, pp. 118–125.

Porfiri, Aurelio (2017). "*Musicam Sacram*: Fifty Years of a Controversial Document." In *Rivista Internazionale di Musica Sacra* 38, pp. 323–334.

——— (2013). *Il canto dei secoli* [*The Song of the Centuries*]. Venice: Marcianum Press.

——— (2017a). *Ci chiedevano parole di canto* [*They Asked Us for Songs*]. Hong Kong: Chorabooks.

——— (2017b). *La Messa in-canto* [*The Mass in Song*]. Hong Kong: Chorabooks.

——— (2018). *Delle cinque piaghe del canto liturgico* [*On the Five Wounds of Liturgical Song*]. Hong Kong: Chorabooks.

——— (2019). *Messa a punto* [*Mass Clarity*]. Hong Kong: Chorabooks.

——— (2020a) *Non ti pago!* [*I Won't Pay You!*]. Hong Kong: Chorabooks.

——— (2020b). *Cantate inni con arte e con suono melodioso* [*Sing Songs with Skill and Melodious Sound*]. Hong Kong: Chorabooks.

——— (2020c). *Forever I Will Sing*. Hong Kong: Catholic Centre Chinese University of Hong Kong.

——— (2021). *Un canto nuovo* [*A New Song*]. Hong Kong: Chorabooks.

——— (2022a). *Che musica maestro?* [*What Music, Maestro?*]. Hong Kong: Chorabooks.

——— (2022b). *Un grande future alle spalle* [*A Grand Future behind Us*]. Hong Kong: Chorabooks.

——— (2022c). *Sing to the Lord.* Hong Kong: Spring Publications Limited (Chinese Version).

——— (2023). *Ci hanno detto* [*They Told Us*]. Hong Kong: Chorabooks.

Porfiri, Aurelio, and Aldo Maria Valli (2018). *Sradicati* [*Uprooted*]. Hong Kong: Chorabooks.

Ratzinger, Joseph (1985). "Liturgy and Sacred Music." In *Christus in Ecclesia Cantat.* Edited by J. Overath. Rome: CIMS, 47–60.

——— (1986). *The Feast of Faith: Approaches to a Theology of the Liturgy.* San Francisco: Ignatius Press.

——— (1997a). *Salt of the Earth: The Church at the End of the Millennium; An Interview with Peter Seewald.* Cinisello Balsamo: San Paolo.

——— (1997b). *Milestones: Memoirs (1927–1977).* Cinisello Balsamo: Editrice San Paolo.

——— (2001). *The Spirit of the Liturgy.* San Francisco: Ignatius Press.

——— (2006). *Dare bellezza per la gloria di Dio: discorso alla Cappella musicale pontificia Sistina* [*Give Beauty for the Glory of God: Discourse to the Pontifical Sistine Musical Chapel*]. Panzano in Chianti: Feeria, Comunità di San Leolino.

——— (2010). *Opera omnia.* Vol. 11: *Liturgical Theology.* Città del Vaticano.

Benedetto XVI (2023). *Che cos'è il cristianesimo: Quasi un testamento spirituale* [*What Is Christianity? A Sort of Spiritual Testament*]. Edited by Elio Guerriero and Georg Gänswein. Milan: Mondadori.

Rossen, Jane Mink (1978). "The Suahongi of Bellona: Polynesian Ritual Music." In *Ethnomusicology* 22.3, pp. 397–439.

Sander, Ernest H. (2001). "Hocket." In *Grove Music Online*. https://www.oxfordmusiconline.com/grovemusic/view/10.1093/gmo/9781561592630.001.0001/omo-9781561592630-e-0000013115. Oxford University Press.

Schmidt, K. L. (1969). "κύμβαλον." In *The Great Lexicon of the New Testament*. Italian edition edited by F. Montagnini, Giuseppe Scarpat, and O. Soffritti. *Vol. 5*. Edited by Gerhard Kittel and Gerhard Freidrich. Brescia: Paideia, coll. 1336–1340.

Schneider, Athanasius, and Porfiri Aurelio (2022). *The Catholic Mass: Steps to Restore the Centrality of God in the Liturgy.* Manchester, NH: Sophia Institute Press.

Schneider, Marius (1962). "Râga-Maqam-Nomos." In *Die Musik in Geschichte und Gegenwart*. Vol. 10. Kassel: Bärenreiter, pp. 1864–1868.

——— (1999). *Il significato della musica* [*The Meaning of Music*]. Milan: Rusconi.

Scruton, Roger (2009). *Beauty*. Oxford, Oxford University Press.

Senior, John (1978). *The Death of Christian Culture*. New Rochelle, NY: Arlington House.

——— (2008). *The Restoration of Christian Culture*. Norfolk, VA: IHS Press.

Siri, Giuseppe (1978). *Pastorali quaresimali*. Genova.

Staglianò, Antonio (2018). *Pop-theology per giovani: Autocritica del cattolicesimo convezionale per un cristianesimo umano* [*Pop Theology for Young People: Self-Criticism of Traditional Catholicism for a Human Christianity*]. Introduction by Antonio Spadaro. Soveria Mannelli: Rubbettino.

——— (2020). *Sulle note di Dio: Pop-theology per far scoprire ai giovani la bellezza della fede* [*On the Notes of God: Pop Theology for Helping*

Young People Discover the Beauty of Faith]. Introduction by Francesco Cosentino. Soveria Mannelli: Rubbettino.

Tagliaferri, Roberto (2009). *La tazza rotta: Il rito; Risorsa dimenticata dell'umanità* [*The Broken Cup: The Rite; A Forgotten Resource of Humanity*]. Padua: Messaggero.

Tylor, Edward Burnett (1871). *Primitive Culture: Research into the Development of Mythology, Philosophy, Religion, Art, and Custom.* Third ed. London: John Murray.

Werner, Eric (1959). *The Sacred Bridge: The Interdependence of Liturgy and Music in Synagogue and Church during the First Millennium.* New York: Columbia University Press.

Windisch, Hans (1967). "Ἕλλην, Ἑλλάς, Ἑλληνικός, Ἑλληνίς, Ἑλληνιστής, Ἑλληνιστί." In *The Great Lexicon of the New Testament.* Italian edition edited by F. Montagnini, Giuseppe Scarpat, and O. Soffritti. *Vol. 3.* Edited by Gerhard Kittel and Gerhard Freidrich. Brescia: Paideia, coll. 469–504.

About the Authors

AURELIO PORFIRI is an Italian composer, conductor, educator, and writer. He is a renowned expert in sacred music and a scholar on China and Catholic traditionalism. He is the author of *The Right Hand of the Lord Is Exalted* and the co-author, with Bishop Athanasius Schneider, of the bestselling *The Catholic Mass*, already translated in multiple languages. He is a contributor to major Catholic and conservative blogs in Italy, France, and the United States. The popular American magazine *Inside the Vatican* included him in the top ten most influential people in 2021.

BISHOP ATHANASIUS SCHNEIDER is one of the foremost defenders of Catholic orthodoxy today. He is a prolific author and serves as auxiliary bishop of the Archdiocese of St. Mary in Astana, Kazakhstan, chairman of the Liturgical Commission, and secretary-general of the Conference of Catholic Bishops of Kazakhstan. He is the author of many books, including *The Springtime That Never Came*, *The Catholic Mass*, *Flee from Heresy*, and the most current and engaging catechism of our time, *Credo: Compendium of the Catholic Faith.*

GUIDO MILANESE is a respected scholar with a deep understanding of the historical and cultural contexts of sacred music. His contributions provide a rich backdrop to the ongoing dialogue about the role of music in worship.

Sophia Institute

Sophia Institute is a nonprofit institution that seeks to nurture the spiritual, moral, and cultural life of souls and to spread the gospel of Christ in conformity with the authentic teachings of the Roman Catholic Church.

Sophia Institute Press fulfills this mission by offering translations, reprints, and new publications that afford readers a rich source of the enduring wisdom of mankind.

Sophia Institute also operates the popular online resource CatholicExchange.com. *Catholic Exchange* provides world news from a Catholic perspective as well as daily devotionals and articles that will help readers to grow in holiness and live a life consistent with the teachings of the Church.

In 2013, Sophia Institute launched Sophia Institute for Teachers to renew and rebuild Catholic culture through service to Catholic education. With the goal of nurturing the spiritual, moral, and cultural life of souls, and an abiding respect for the role and work of teachers, we strive to provide materials and programs that are at once enlightening to the mind and ennobling to the heart; faithful and complete, as well as useful and practical.

Sophia Institute gratefully recognizes the Solidarity Association for preserving and encouraging the growth of our apostolate over the course of many years. Without their generous and timely support, this book would not be in your hands.

www.SophiaInstitute.com
www.CatholicExchange.com
www.SophiaTeachers.org